RENDEZVOUS
WITH THE
INVISIBLES

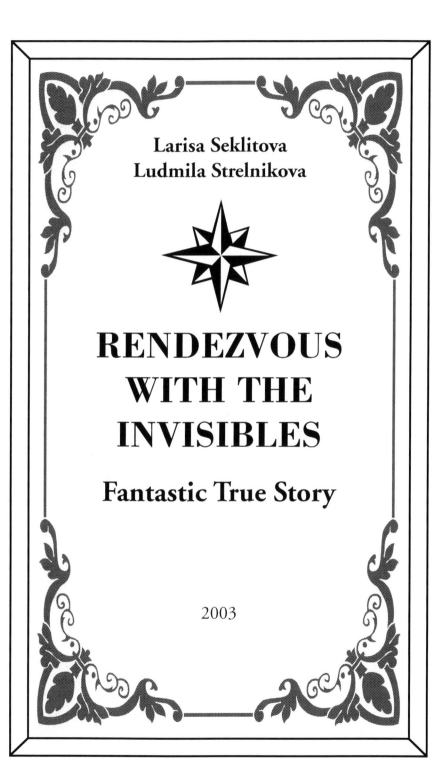

Larisa Seklitova
Ludmila Strelnikova

RENDEZVOUS WITH THE INVISIBLES

Fantastic True Story

2003

Larisa Seklitova, Ludmila Strelnikova, 2003.

RENDEZVOUS WITH THE INVISIBLES
«Beyond the Bounds of Unknown» series.

Translator – Calin Jardan

This book is about unusual meetings of the authors with representatives from other worlds, about penetration of the person into other dimensions and establishment of contacts with living beings from other civilizations.

Order this book online at www.trafford.com
or email orders@trafford.com

Most Trafford titles are also available at major online book retailers.

Printed in the United States of America.

ISBN: 978-1-4269-7097-9 (sc)
ISBN: 978-1-4269-7098-6 (e)

Trafford rev. 05/25/2011

 www.trafford.com

North America & International
toll-free: 1 888 232 4444 (USA & Canada)
phone: 250 383 6864 ♦ fax: 812 355 4082

TABLE OF CONTENTS

Larisa Seklitova, Ludmila Strelnikova.

RENDEZVOUS WITH THE INVISIBLES

Foreword

Scientists search for traces of other civilizations in Space using telescopes and radars, study radiations of quasars and pulsars, checking whether they come from an artificial source which has been created by other civilization and sends now to us signals which we cannot decipher.

All searches occur basically in a radio range, which is accessible to perception by existing devices.

Scientists consider that signals of an artificial origin should be in well studied by them spectrum of frequencies. But who has told them, that others should talk in the same spectrum? Who has limited them by frameworks of their own matter?

It is necessary to search in other range.

Aliens fly here under our very nose, but in other spectrum energy, however we are looking for them millions light years away from us, although it's enough to give a hand to make friendly hand shake. They sing to us melodies of their worlds, but we as deaf-mutes, are not able to hear their wonderful singing.

And so to be sure of it, it is enough only to create the devices working with frequencies energy of the subtle world. Then the window in the adjacent world, where we will see many living beings surpassing us by the level of development, will be flung wide open.

Entrance to the subtle world is provided by not only devices, but also by your own development. The person comes nearer to the Higher civilizations of the subtle plane rising step by step based on his/her own improvement.

To communicate with the subtle world one should ripen to learn to understand them as fellows in your own world. And we lead readers to follow in our footsteps through numerous channelings so that they could together with us rise on a higher level of knowledge and see what we have seen, and accept by heart that what we have accepted.

Alexander Strelnikov

Introduction

Before telling about our meetings with aliens, I would like to make some general explanations on the basis of that knowledge which has been received by us later on.

The majority of people do not believe in aliens because they cannot see them. The person got used to consider that all rational beings should be similar to him/her as the carrier of the higher intelligence what he/she think about him/herself. But there are incredible amount of reasonable forms in our Universe, and their configurations are so unusual for consciousness of the man that he can stand near the living being and will not take it for a reasonable state.

A form of living being is created for a world, for those energies which it consists of and which they should transform. That is the reason of construction features appearance and strangeness of their designs.

There are material and subtle beings. In subtle worlds they are also subdivided into many kinds, however some of them has the form accessible to perception by our clairvoyants, but some forms belong to a range of energies, which are not perceived by any human organs, feelings.

Actually the man can divide aliens into two types: visible and invisible. Visible ones, i.e. having the material form, not all possess precisely the same physical body, as well as the person. In their worlds they exist in one form, but in our world they must be similar to the human not to shock by their unusual appearance. That is such aliens are able to materialize and own codes of the physical matter.

Therefore they show themselves in a human appearance, freely walk among people. However, they can only walk about. They are not able to establish human relations and apply behavior rules in society to the full extent, as they have their own norms and interaction rules with each other. It is possible to find them out by some strangenesses in their behavior. However there are also beings on other planets, completely similar to the man, and there are a lot of them.

But why do material worlds have different forms although, it seems there would be the only one enough, universal to distribute it everywhere in the whole Universe? As things turned out, the physical matter has different Levels of development, and it means that it has a certain power potential and parameters which differ from indicators of our matter. Besides, every world is calculated on living in it souls of certain power potential and might, which necessarily correspond to the power potential of that matter, in which they are moved into. Therefore many highly developed souls from highly developed material worlds, i.e. the souls having accumulated in their development high power potential, are not able to be incarnated in human bodies. These bodies are low potential and if to incarnate in them highly potential souls, they will simply blow up or burn down. Human bodies will burst like soap bubbles. Therefore, when aliens with highly potential soul arrive in our inferior world, they are materialized in bodies corresponding to the requirements of their souls. And thus necessarily enter a protective field, which for a human eye remains invisible, but protects them from negative influences of our environment. Everyone arriving to us has its own system of protection. Also time parameters are necessarily connected. Aliens are able to use it, but the man takes it for a fairy tale. However time has the secrets of its own, and highly developed beings are able to manage it. These are the peculiarities of aliens' appearance in our world.

However, more often they prefer to shield from the man with the protective field doing invisible not only them, but also spaceships. They do not come into contact with the man, because they consider it low. They are not interested in savages, so to say. In our world they carry out a certain work charged by God, and have no right to do other actions as they are subordinated by *the Law of non-interference*, operating in all Universe. As I have already written in the book «Secrets of Higher Worlds», all of them arrive to the Earth to carry out special work under the contract with God, as our Spiritual Systems are not able to perform it themselves, because Entities (Higher beings from Hierarchy) are made of a subtle matter, which can penetrate in our rough world. Entities will pass through us like through air. And when, for example, moving of tectonic plates in a material world or any other work are needed, then material "hands", material tools of influence are required.

For realization of some works on the Earth aliens often send robots calculated on a physical matter of our Level. And, naturally they do robots which are similar more often to the form of the man, the provement of it is numerous cases of meetings humanoids with people described in the press.

There are a lot of aliens on the Earth from the subtle world. They also have different forms, but there are some who are similar to the human. The density of their subtle matter is different. And if their bodies correspond to the etheric, astral plane of our Earth they become visible for clairvoyants.

Depending on the Level of development of clairvoyants they are capable to see beings from the different worlds: some – beings from the low world, others – from high. The man never takes into account the development level of clairvoyants, although it has a great value in evidences given by them. If to set such an experiment: take two clairvoyants – of a low development Level and high, sit in one room and offer them to concentrate on the subtle world and then to inform us what they see. The low level clairvoyant will see devils, and high – angels (I, of course, give symbolical examples to make it more clear). Thus, there is a law-governed nature of connection: each individual depending on Level of the development is connected to that subtle world, which corresponds to him. And only people of identical Level can see the same subtle world and give similar evidences. Although if to consider that everyone possesses individual perception of the world, in such a case they, seeing the same, will describe it differently. And as the result it is impossible to get from people absolutely identical images of objects from the subtle world.

At the same time basing on what the man sees, one can judge about the degree of his soul maturity. Evolutionary a young soul cannot connect to a high Level and see its construction. But a high individual can see the low worlds, which he has overcome before, they are open to his perception. All works in harmony.

In our earthly world there are many beings of the subtle plane . It is not required for them to protect artificially from the man by any shielding field because an ordinary human does not see them. They can freely walk about in our apartments and observe us. They are able even to pass through us, and we will not notice it. Such beings may come from earthly parallel worlds, and can arrive from the subtle worlds of other planets. They are harmless to the man, because everybody who arrives, possesses a high Level of development, and as a consequence, high ethics of behavior, or in earthly language, high moral qualities. They do not arrange to the man dirty tricks and do not play a joke on him although it's quite possible for them. Their high morals do not accept disrespectful relation to a representative of other world.

Even though there are cases of penetration into the earthly world of beings from aggressive planes. They can hurt separate people. But these are single cases. Basically aliens bring peace. So we are surrounded by many invisible beings, and in the majority they are representatives of subtle worlds.

Several times my Heavenly Teacher allowed me looking at the earthly world not with a physical sight, but with astral. The show was incredible: the sky was shining not because of subtle radiations of stars, but with fires of unearthly ships. There were multitude of them. Huge, majestic, in the light of flickering fires, of the most freakish forms, they were easily moving, as it seemed to me, in our sky despite I saw another plane of existence. But in this amazing show I felt very accurately the power and grandeur of these spaceships. There was something great, mysterious and beautiful in them.

Therefore, to see flying ships of aliens, it is necessary to concentrate on frequency of their energy. Subtle worlds conceal infinite amount of secrets and mysteries, but our imperfect equipment does not allow revealing them. Thus, our scientists face the issue of the prompt creation of devices, which could be tuned on energy frequencies of subtle worlds. Such devices will help to see a lot of surprising even from a surface of the Earth. It is time to make friends with the subtle world, instead of imagining it as a crowd of monsters from human mind.

*   *   *

Now we are passing to a meeting with our aliens. We have already had channelings with the Higher space Systems "the Union" and have received the first knowledge about that non-material world, which is behind the bounds of human perception.

As we formed new concepts, so we got acquainted with sort of unusual phenomena and beings of the non-material nature. Long before the beginning of channelings we had been brought to comprehension of existence of subtle world by means of spiritualistic sessions. My sisters suddenly found out abilities of mediums, and they began to communicate with souls of the dead. And then for the first time behind the bounds of our material ideas we saw another world invisible to us. The world from where others could influence us and find any ways of dialogue. They tried to learn more about us from that world, and we tried to learn more about them...

Then channelings began, at first unpretentious and naive, typical for beginners. Meanwhile we were allowed to be engaged in practical work, to do all possible investigations of the subtle plane. Then we were given the possibility to "study" also the souls belonging to other subtle worlds, therefore from human souls study in 1992 we passed to acquaintance with the souls developing in other worlds.

While teaching, they created situations, where we faced with many mysterious cases and facts. We should not only accept them as real-life, breaking our former material believes, but also to understand them, comprehend and carry out something new to ourselves.

We passed space universities where there were both the theory, and practice, passed space exams. It was necessary not only to understand what is beyond the human perception, but also connect it with a material basis of the world, to learn joining the old with the new, but at the same time not to transform the first into dogmas, and the second – in illusion. The main thing was – to learn to connect one with another, to unite together grains of true sprouts and to reject tares in the form of incorrect theories and hypotheses which have bred the great variety by this time. It was necessary to wake in ourselves the ability to see new and to perceive it as a drink of pure air, but not that bomb which can destroy everything.

Therefore our meeting with aliens was educational. Its purpose was to learn communicating with beings from other worlds and from the informative point of view to reveal something new; to compare our worlds, and also living beings by the form and the way of life. We need to understand what they see and understand our world not as the man does, but absolutely the other way round in our own way.

Chapter 1

The first meeting

Our meeting with aliens took place in the end of 1992. At this time we had a new channeler –a young man Dmitry.

He got acquainted with daughter Larisa and began to visit us. And as he faced a zone of high energies in our apartment, that was why his abilities of clairvoyance and clairaudience started to show up. I want to notice here that any human abilities reveal temporarily under the influence of stresses, high energies or other factors. If the man does not use them constantly, they disappear. They also can be closed while changing of environment factors. Therefore Dmitry's abilities revealed only for a while when he was working with us.

Dmitry, as well as the daughter, was twenty years old at that time. The young man was completely unaware of channelings, subtle worlds and existence in them other beings. He led a simple life of the provincial and had never thought that once he would face the unusual. But after several visits to our apartment he began to notice strangenesses in himself.

One day when he came over to us, he told:

– "Today I was walking along the central street, looking under my feet and suddenly saw – there, underground, not clearly on what depth red stones were shining as if they were burning. Like the precious ones. I saw it for a short instant, and then all disappeared. What is it – it's not clear for me."

– There were four of us in the room: he with our daughter Larisa and my husband and I – Alexander Strelnikov.

– "You could see magma in interior of the Earth," – supposed my husband, – "there could be such minutes of enlightenment."

– " Is it really so close to a surface?" – the young man was surprised.

– "No, magma is deeply near the nucleus of the Earth. Simply you have seen far away," –answered Alexander.

– "But will not there be eruption?" – ingenuously smiling, assumed Dmitry. – "It seemed to me that it was very close to the surface. To tell you the truth, I thought that found the treasure with rubies. They resembles precious stones, but with lighting," – and he started to laugh, having understood impossibility of the made assumption.

– "Where will you see underground the lighting? Only from magma," –affirmatively declared Alexander. – "But, I think eruption will not happen, while we are here. So, my friend, there are no rubies here. Although I have another guess – peat could smoulder underground. It burns beautifully, pieces of coal blaze and shine, as jewels."

Next time, sitting with us in a room and talking, Dmitry also found out in himself some strangenesses.

Larisa came to another room and closed behind a plywood door. Dmitry silently looked at the door some time and then puzzled a bit informed:

– "For some reason I see Larisa through the closed door and through the wall. She is looking for a book in her room on the shelf. I cannot understand – what is happening with my eyes?"

I begun smiling:

– "The third eye opens. Enjoy it. Abilities to clairvoyance reveal. Now you will see through walls, and look in stomachs of people – know who and what has eaten," – I was kidding.

– "It is interesting," – Dmitry was delighted. –"and I do not understand what happens with me. I am not drunk, and goodness knows what fancies.

Larisa entered the room with a book in her hands that proved what Dmitry had seen. She offered him the book:

– "If you have time, read it. It is called – «The Third Eye». This book is about, how one boy was trying to reveal abilities to clairvoyance."

– "And what do I need it to show up for? I have already revealed," –boasted Dmitry.

– "When abilities reveal before understanding, the man can go mad or do himself harm," –said Larisa.

– "Yes, he has abilities," – I agreed, – "but how could they be developed further and how to direct them into a necessary trend?"

– "Let's experiment," – offered Larisa, having taken a seat in an armchair hardly little bit away from the young man.

– "Yes, there is nothing we enjoy better than experimenting," – Alexander joked and addressed to Dmitry: – "Are you ready to take part in experiments?"

–"Yes," – he agreed immediately, without even understanding, in what he should "participate". And only after having agreed, showed an interest: – "And what should I do?"

–"You see with open eyes, and they divert you. Close them and try to concentrate your attention in the centre of the forehead," – offered my husband.

The young man obediently closed his eyes, but saw nothing.

– "Darkness. Only some stains are floating before eyes," – he said.

– "Look with your forehead, try to imagine that energy is gathering in the centre," – adjusted Alexander.

Smiling, I observed attempts of the future clairvoyant but as it was in vain I offered the help.

– "Let's concentrate ourselves. We will unite our energy and direct an energy flow to his forehead centre. We only need to ask our Teachers to keep an eye on the experiment and make it harmless."

In our thoughts we addressed to our Teachers asking to concentrate so much energy in a beam, as it needed to achieve the opening of the third eye and would not cause harm to Dmitry. Surpluses of energy could be injurious for his health. Norm is required everywhere; any overdose is dangerous as when you take medicine: a certain dose treats, and surpluses turn to poison.

Without Teachers it is impossible to carry out such experiments. We only began the researches and much yet did not understand operation of subtle energies, therefore all should be controlled by Them.

After having received a signal that experiment was allowed, we started to act. The beam went. Dmitry continued to sit with closed eyes. Three minutes later while concentrating the beam on him, he told:

– "It is getting lighter ... Stains have left ... It seems, I begin to see clearly, but everything is like in the fog."

– "Concentrate," – Alexander ordered. – "Observe."

– "O-o," – suddenly silently and mysteriously whispered Dmitry,- "apparently, we are not alone here."

– "Whom do you see?" – Larisa showed an interest.

–"Shhh, do not move," – the young man whispered as if was afraid to frighten off a bird on tree branches.

Larisa stood still. We were waiting for the following messages. The young man peered into the picture, which had spread out before him. He saw us in a strange for him luminescence. Our bodies were as if were contained in shining gas ovals. Having become foggy and having lost clearness, we flickered and shone everyone in his own spectrum with one prevailing tint. Larisa shone with white light, me tinged with gentle-pink, Alexander – with yellow light.

But not our light excited Dmitry, because every man shines in the subtle plane, but everyone – in his/her own way. The Young man saw those two strangers who, having squatted down, were in front of Larisa and were attentively examining her. The third alien stood apart.

– "There are three more in the room," – in a whisper informed Dmitry. – "they are a bit strange: look like people, and do not look like."

At this moment one of the aliens, who was squatting, turned a head towards Dmitry and as it seemed to him, gave him a piercing glance of his burning eyes. He in fear recoiled back, leaning on an armchair back, and with anxiety whispered:

– "He is looking at me."

– "Do not afraid," – I encouraged, already knowing from own experience that it was not necessary to be afraid of those beings, who were not perceived by our physical sight. For two years of channelings we had not heard, that they did somebody harm.

– "It needs to contact with them and talk," – I offered.

– "It's interesting, do they hear us?" – thoughtfully asked the daughter.

– "Hardly. As they are from the other world, their hearing organ should be adapted on other frequencies," – I explained. – "but how can we talk to them? What language?"

The issue was difficult. It was necessary to find a way of communication. They were in the subtle world, we – in physical. They, however, saw us and even could examine, but we could perceive them only through the channeler.

To talk with a help of some signs, mimicry, gestures was useless. For this purpose we need to know their way of life, and to it – ours. To speak, it seemed to us, was useless. If we do not understand our foreigners speaking their languages we will not understand also these beings. Moreover, it could appear that they like snakes or fish, are not able to use sound communication.

– "Perhaps let's try telepathy," –offered Alexander. – "Let Dmitry send them questions."

– "I cannot transfer thoughts, and even do not know what is it," – whispered the channeler and added concerning the seen: – "One continues looking at me. Maybe, he has suspected something. Oh, what big eyes he has. What should I do?

–"Tell them that we are glad to see them here at home and we wish to get acquainted," – I suggested to him.

Dmitry transferred, and, strangely enough, they understood him. Both recovered feet and answered, that were also not against to get acquainted with us.

They introduced themselves. One named Edar, the second – Los, the third – Fit. All three looked like people, had the same appearance form, however, the skin did not look soft, but was firm, metal, and had a silver-violet shade. They were dressed in body close fit dark blue overalls. Their figures were different. Fit was thin, but well-knit. Edar had athletic body build and was high. But the face looked thin. A bit longish, with slightly hollow cheeks, it was prettified by the big burning eyes. It seemed fire was burning in them. The long face was framed with the long dark hair going down a little below shoulders and doing him romantic fashion.

Los opposed to him was small and thick. He did not reach even Edar's shoulder. A round face was prettified only by little eyes, because he had not hair at all. But despite lacking of separate details, in general he made pleasant impression, looked quiet, good-natured, and, obviously, it was his main advantage. I do not describe Fit particularly, because he has not appeared any more.

To basic distinctive features of strangers, besides the skin, it was possible to add quantity of fingers on their hands (there were seven of them on each hand, and they were of an identical length) and flipper-like feet.

We introduced ourselves too. Acquaintance took place. As for us, of course, we were interested, how they understood our language.

– "Have you studied Russian?" – I asked through the channeler.
–"There are plenty of languages on the Earth. How do you understand them?"

Los answered. Obviously, he was senior among them.

– "We do not study language, as we perceive concepts, images arising in the human brain."

– "Do you understand every person?"

– "No. We do not understand you directly. A translator, as Dmitry, is necessary for us. He has a special construction, which allows connecting you and us. It is for the first time when we meet such translator on the Earth. We like him."

– "Where are you from?" –asked Alexander.

– "The name of our planet will tell nothing to people. An empty phrase. We can say only that it is one of the planets in Sirius constellation, the third parallel world. We are from it."

– "Have you such material beings like people on your planet?" – I was interested.

– "No. For your sight it is deserted. Beings live in other dimension, than the material body of the planet. But here we also have met many beings, which are in other dimension too."

– "Have you met here people in parallel worlds?" – I tried to get more details.

– "No, people - they are similar to you. Every world has its own beings. They have another structure and name. We also resemble you, but we are not people."

– "Not people," - Larisa repeated and unexpectedly asked: - "But do you have the same structure inside you as we have?"

Los was going to answer, but Edar, who had kept silence was ahead.

– "We have not examined internal structure of the man yet, but we know that living beings in their construction are different as they are intended for different purposes. Yesterday, when we were flying by one earthly place, we saw a being, which did not look like the human. It was sinking in the water. We rescued it, but it escaped from us."

– "Please, describe it" – Larisa was curious, trying to understand, whom they had met.

– "The being was covered with short hair, there were sharp sticks on the head. It had four limbs, but we found no hands among them," - Edar described shortly.

– "Maybe, it was a goat or a deer," – decided Larisa, addressing to us with the assumption. – "horns he took for sticks."

The fact that our mysterious visitors had rescued a living being made us well disposed towards them. Before this story we had felt tension, knowing nothing what to wait from them. Basing on our earthly experience we knew very well that words did not always serve as soul characteristics. Only acts are capable to characterize it precisely.

– "Why were you examining Larisa? Do you see the man for the first time?" –I showed an interest. – "We would like to know, how do you perceive people visually? We, for example, do not see and hear you. Without the channeler you do not exist for us."

– "Your girl has an interesting structure, we have not seen such yet. And she is sparkling with white light. I like it very much," - explained Edar, having answered the first part of my questions. Los answered the second one.

– "We have passed longer evolutionary way of development, therefore we see either your material bodies, or those, which are in other dimension. Do you know that you are present in several dimensions?" – He addressed to us.

– "No," - we frankly admitted our ignorance and tried to justify. – "we only begin to study a subtle structure of the man."

– "And what purpose did you arrive to the Earth for?" – asked Alexander.

– "There are a lot of purposes," - answered Los. –" We, for example, are interested in new devices. By the way, is it possible to rummage here in this box?" – He pointed at our new TV with the decoder. – "I would like to draw a scheme from it."

Being afraid that after they would "rummage" in our new TV, we would need to bring it to a repair shop, I offered them an old one, which was in the room of my daughter.

– "There is the same device in the second room. You may take it to pieces. We can even present it to you."

– "No, we are interested in this one," - insinuatingly, but persistently said Los, and explained: - "There is such a feature in it which is not present in other box."

They needed the decoder, as we understood, because it was the detail that made difference in comparison of both TVs. We grudged the new TV, but how could we refuse our visitors? And we graciously agreed.

– "Well, rummage," - I nodded.

But the only one TV was not enough. Los politely asked:

– "Is it possible for us to rummage in a white box which hangs on your wall in the next room?" – I understood that it was a question about the radio. – "your box emits the same sound, as the man. If we study it out, we could make for ourselves the device responding to a human voice. We will hear the person at very big distances."

– "Please, study," - Alexander agreed. The third member of the team immediately came to the kitchen where a white box of a wall loud-speaker hung, and we said him goodbye in our thoughts. Everything was for the sake of dear visitors from other world.

– "What did you fly to us?" – asked Alexander.

– "Spaceship."

– "What form does it have?"

– "Oval. But along the edges outside there are a lot of all possible gears. There are antennas absorbing energy from your Sun or other stars during the flight."

– "And where did you leave it?"

– "It is above your house right now. But it is invisible for people."

– "What kind of fuel does it use for flight?"

– "Our ship works on two types of energy. One type is the basic and the second – auxiliary. It is just – energy of stars, your Sun. When our ship is located near some star, we use its energy but when we leave it we pass to the reserve type of fuel," - willingly explained Los.

The channeler having cheerfully translated conversation between us and aliens, suddenly silently whispered to Alexander:

– "Hide an alarm clock. Slowly go up to it, take and hide. Edar is looking at it for some reason. They will now put all your household appliances out of operation."

Alexander obediently stood up and, doing an easy appearance, went up to the wall where the alarm clock was ticking on the shelf. First of all he shielded it with his back, then imperceptibly as it seemed to him, put one hand behind a back, took the alarm clock and slowly put it in his trouser pocket. It was possible to stay without TV, radio, but without an alarm clock – in any way impossible, because all the family used it to wake up for a work.

This time Larisa, trying to divert attention of visitors to herself, asked Los:

– "For what purpose do you need our TV? Are you going to make the same devices on your planet?"

When the daughter began asking, this romantic from Sirius, Edar took the initiative to answer her. I nicknamed him romantic for long hair, big burning and at the same time thoughtful eyes. Subsequently this name was proved to be true.

– "There is a device in your apparatus, which suits us for one invention. On the basis of it we want to make the device for country video shooting. Then it will be possible to look through all around on a special screen, everything which is outside of the ship."

– "Don't you see it indeed?" – Larisa was surprised. – "Probably, there are windows and any navigating equipment, aren't they?"

– "Similar devices are, but their construction, from our point of view, is not successful enough. We constantly improve equipment."

Meanwhile Alexander came back his place. The alarm clock was ticking in his pocket.

– "Can you become visible for us?" – asked Larisa again.

– "Sometimes we can. But for this purpose a lot of energy is required. However, when people see us, they are always frightened," - answered Edar.

– "Is it because you are very terrible?" – asked directly the daughter.

– "We are not terrible, simply for the man - unusual. We are handsome on the whole," – kindly said Edar.

– "We would like to see you. What handsome you are," - the daughter smiled.

– "Somehow another time," - the alien promised. – "we like you, we wish to come to you one more time. Will you allow us to come, when we shall have free time?"

– "We are always glad to see you," - Larisa affably answered and asked with the interest: - "And have you got women on the ship?"

– "We have".

– "Then come with them."

– "We have only one. Well, we will introduce her to you," - promised Edar.

– "And how did you get to our apartment?" – I asked. – "there are plenty of families in our house, and you appeared here."

We lived in a big nine-floor house, therefore they had many variants whom to visit. But they for some reason got to us.

– "We moved to light. In comparison with other people you shine more," - answered Los. – "your lightning is seen far away and it drew our attention first of all. And, besides, we have heard wonderful music. Larisa was playing some instrument. All this made us visit your dwelling."

Our daughter liked to play the electronic piano during her spare minutes. Usually she retired in her room and played only for herself. The instrument produced bewitching sounds, and they, as appeared, did not remain unnoticed even for aliens.

– "And did earthly music attract you?" – I was surprised. – "Probably, you have absolutely another kind of music on your planet? Even the man does not like any music, and some seems intolerable. Has the earthly music seemed really foreign for you?"

– "Yes, we know that music may be unpleasant. But that one, which was being reproduced by Larisa, was consonant to our soul," - answered Los. – "Music is developed and on our planet, we love it, especially Edar. We do not perceive human speech …" - he made a pause for some seconds and added: - "for a while, but music is a special sounding, special energy. It sounds in many worlds in which we have been. But there are worlds without music. Edar collects melodies of different planets. Let Larisa play on her instrument. It was pleasure for us to listen to her. We wish to listen attentively, understand, what peculiarities earthly melodies possess."

Wishing to favorably impress the visitors and at the same time divert them from household appliances, Larisa sat down at the electronic piano – and wonderful sounds filled the room. A touching melody was flowing from her slender fingers, filling soul with pressing grief and carrying it away in the unknown world of unfounded hopes. Sounds were spreading over the room in silvery streams, fascinating and immersing in memories.

For some time, listening to a melody, we had diverted from the aliens. And when Dmitry looked at our visitors he could not restrain exclamation:

– "Look!" – However, he exclaimed hushfully as if trying that they did not hear him.

– "What's up?" – We begun to worry. – "What happens?"

Dmitry in a whisper began to comment on the seen.

– "Both of them are crying, and in the way that tears do not simply fall, but flow in streams. I have never seen such tears before. Where is so much from? They are flowing directly to their boilersuits and to the floor … Oho!" – exclaimed soon. – "There is even a pool on the floor. They will flood us right now," - he told in uneasy whisper.

– "Perhaps it is necessary to stop to play, what do you think? Ask them," - I began to worry.

Dmitry translated to them, but they protested:

– "Let her play. We have recollected our home, our planet. We have not seen them for a long time."

Their nostalgia was clear to us. Aliens as appeared were very sensitive; we did not expect it from them.

Larisa played three melodies and, having turned to us, joked:

– "That's enough, otherwise their longing for home will overwhelm, and they will depart, without having carried out their the task."

Aliens were satisfied with that what had been played, and thanked:

– "Thank you for the music. You lighted up our souls. So it is pleasant to listen to earthly sounds. You know, Edar is the musician, too," - informed Los about the companion. – He had had a fine instrument at home, too, and he often played it. But there was an attack of aggressive inhabitants of the planet 266 on us. Our houses were destroyed, and the instrument – too. Your melodies caused in us sad memories. Sorry."

We felt uneasiness that we made them suffer and caused such splash of emotions in them.

Larisa guilty said:

– "If I knew that they had reacted in such a way, I would have played something more cheerful."

– "Do you have wars, too?" – I addressed to Los. – "We have thought that if you are technically highly developed, you have no wars."

– "We ourselves never carry on war, only defend. Our planet is very peaceful. But the neighboring planet on the contrary – is aggressive. Attacks happen from their side."

– "How do you defend yourself?" – asked Alexander.

– "We protect all our planet energetically. But when inhabitants of the planet 266 accumulate more energy, than we have, they manage to break through our protection. And then they make destructions and capture our riches. After that again fly away to their planet. They cannot stay on our planet for a long time because they exist in other range of frequencies."

– "Does it mean, that living beings are killed on your planet, too?" – said Alexander.

– "No, there is another tactics. We never kill, and they also do not kill. They take prisoner our beings, but we are able to neutralize them, that is we do not kill, we neutralize."

– "How do you do it?"

– "We have a special apparatus. It gives radiations which are calculated on suppression of enemy motive activity. The enemy is temporarily as though paralyzed."

– "What does it mean temporarily?"

– "Converting into your earthly time – ten or fifteen hours. During this time we go far away or carry them away. We neutralize enemies, then gather all of them and carry away to some place where they come to the senses. But it is just a demonstration of our power. And if they manage to make destructions here, so then it is a demonstration of their superiority."

– "So it means, when you departed from your planet, there had been a war before, hadn't it?" – asked the daughter.

– "It had been a bit earlier. But we are forced to be ready for new attacks constantly. Therefore we went as we were assigned to gather new technical inventions for strengthening of the protection."

– "Do you unless invent nothing?"

– "We invent. But now it is necessary to collect everything in the shortest terms that can be useful to us for defense. It takes long time for inventions and big means, however we have not them. We do not know, when will it take in their head to attack us next time. That is why we have to borrow something in other civilizations. But we borrow not everything, and only separate details, fragments. Then we invent from them something new. Your box," - Los pointed at our TV, - "does not fit us entirely. In our world it will not work, because there is another type of the matter there, not the same environment and this device is calculated on another beings. And from details and fragments we take some principle of work and basing on it do inventions for our world."

– " Are you good at equipment?"

– "Yes, we are able to do much. When you fly your spaceship to other worlds, it is necessary to know much, otherwise you will not survive and die. Therefore we study everything what is possible. We saw here on your Earth many fiddling about beings. We have not such. All free time everyone uses on studying of useful for the future affairs."

– "Could we ask, what hobbies do you have? What is your favorite occupation?"

– "We are concerned with creation of big flying machines and small too. We construct so much, are fascinated with some equipment, produce different devices. Some of them, which are on our ship, we have made ourselves."

At this time Fit returned to the room, and Los declared:

– "It is time for us to depart. We have some deals in other hemisphere of the planet. But we shall return. We were glad to meet you. It's pleasure to find beings on another planet who understand you."

Los raised a half-bent hand upwards so that the palm stopped at shoulder level. Fingers were clenched in a fist. The channeler translated:

– "They say good-bye to you. The clenched fist means that they will return, and when the palm is opened also fingers upwards means they depart forever."

We said goodbye. How aliens rose on their ship, we did not see, because they passed through the wall to neighboring apartment and disappear out of sight. Probably, the flying machine hung not directly over our apartment, but a little aside.

– "At long last, we have got acquainted with aliens," - joyfully exclaimed the daughter. – "now we learn, how other beings behave. Let's give them something as a keepsake," - she suddenly offered. – "I was so sorry when they told that had lost the house and a musical instrument."

– "And how they were crying! If you had just seen," - Dmitry enthusiastically exclaimed. – "I have not seen such yet: tears were running from eyes, as though the crane was opened in each eye."

– "Did they flood the neighbors underneath?" - Larisa was kidding.

– "Do you see remaining pools from their tears?" – asked I.

Dmitry put the third eye into operation, looked and informed:

– "Everything has already evaporated. No traces."

– "How can we know, when they will come again?" – I was thinking of. – "They can appear, but we will not see them.

– "So I have to visit you every day," - Dmitry laughed.

– "Certainly, come," - we agreed. – "You will not burden. We shall have supper together. Now you are responsible for supporting inter-planetary communication."

Chapter 2

Learning general concepts

The next day after work Dmitry straightway came to us and first of all put the third eye into operation. Attentively having examined rooms, he made sure that they were empty.

– "It seems to me, their presence can be determined by biolocational frames," - Alexander thoughtfully supposed. Having studied biolocation, he tried to use it where possible. He got copper frames by means of which he investigated biofields of the man, and informed: - "Next time when they will come, I will try to determine their fields. However they should be shown up somehow in our world."

The idea was interesting. The next day when Dmitry was at work, Alexander and we fell to locate the room. I had metal frames, too, but they were less.

Larisa sat on a sofa and observed, how parents were going about the room with frames in all directions, trying to reveal more concentrated fields. But frames were immovable.

Two days of hunting passed without results. But for the third day, having come for dinner and having eaten in hurry, my husband continued persistently locate. I joked:

– "Now you will devote every free minute to searching for aliens – in what of four corners they have located."

Suddenly frames shuddered and came into operation. Some field was acting in the middle of a room, frames sharply turned in the given place aside as if stroke against something invisible.

– "Take your frames quickly, control," - he asked me. – "It seems to me, there is someone here. Look, how they are moving around." – He walked off for two metres and then began slowly to come closer to the room center. Metal indicators, as upon command, channeled off, testifying the presence of alien fields.

Having heard an emotional voice of the father, Larisa entered the room. She understood right away what the matter was and having extended a hand forward, she tried to feel the field with her own sensations, transforming a palm into a locator.

– "Yes, there is something here, a ball of fire of some field. I feel a slight tingling in fingers," - confirmed she.

My frame struck against something elastic.

– "Perhaps it is some low essence?" - I assumed. – "it is necessary to check up," - and three times crossed the found field then offered the husband: - "Check up now."

This time his frames remained motionless. The field disappeared.

– "Check up all room," – advised Larisa. – "they could move."

He began to examine other places and soon came across the field again in two metres from a former place.

– "Someone changed the place," - he concluded. – "cross it once again."

Larisa and I began to diligently cross an invisible being. The field disappeared again in one place, but appeared in another. Here I explain, what a sign of the cross means, and generally why, as a matter of fact, devils and other evil are afraid of it.

Our fingers radiate streams of energy, and it has already been fixed on pictures made by our scientists. When we join three fingers together to cross we create the powerful stream of energy called a sword of purification. The power of every man is different. A low-developed man may have it very low, therefore not every individual can with his/her sign of the cross frighten away evil.

The beam of energy, coming from three fingers, favorably influences the person when he/she crosses him/herself, because it purifies personal biofield from parasites stuck to subtle bodies. And when the person crosses a low being from the parallel world, then, because of the difference of power potentials of the latter and the person, a beam, like electric mini-discharge, hits this being that is unpleasant and painful for it. Therefore they try to move aside from a sign of the cross.

But in our case it would be possible to make another assumption.

– "Simply it does not like that somebody flourishes arms and pokes with sticks. No, this way we will not define precisely who it is," – I begun to doubt. – "Although it is possible to find out the presence of someone."

– "But who is it? Dead men souls can walk around here, and beings from our parallel worlds, like bogey," – assumed Larisa.

Next day we began to investigate the room again during the lunch time. I speak "lunch", because at this time there was no our channeler, who could check, who is present in the room. In the evening he looked over our apartment, but it was empty. And in the afternoon we over and over again stroke against some fields.

For the second day we found out four fields, i.e. it was possible to assume that there were four beings in the room. One field took place on a chair, the second – on an armchair and two others – on a sofa. In some minutes the field on a chair went away, but appeared near a doorway as though someone moved from a chair to a door.

So casually we found out that the presence of some subtle-material creatures in apartment can be determined with biolocational frames. However such a system did not allow determining, who it was: whether dead men souls, who were many at present, or any other beings of the subtle plane.

We began to worry that we will not see our familiar aliens any more, we will drift apart not, that spatially or in time, but in different dimensions. Being in one point of space at one time, we existed in different dimensions. It served as a barrier to our meeting. However our aliens in this issue, obviously, were more tempted. They knew, that they were to visit us when there was a channeler in the apartment. Therefore one day they appeared in the evening when Dmitry once again was looking over the subtle space of our room.

– "They are," - our translator joyfully exclaimed. "They have come."

– "All three?" – We were delighted.

– "No, two. Edar and Los … They are sending you "hi"."

– "Ask – Have they come to us during a week?"

Dmitry transferred a question and then informed:

– "No. They are here only for the second time."

– "We are glad to their visit. And we ask because someone else visited us, but we could not define, who exactly."

– "As we have noticed, there are many beings in your world whom you do not see. They observe people, but those for them are of no particular interest," – answered Los.

In sincerity of their words concerning that they had not been in our apartment, we did not believe on the whole, as we still knew little about them. They freely could observe us, taking advantage of remaining invisible for us. «Trust, but check» - I remembered a proverb and decided to check up some reasons concerning a sign of the cross.

– "Tell us please, do you have religion?" – I would like to determine, the dark or white Space they belong to and whether they could be frightened of a sign of the cross. «Care will not prevent», decided I.

– "We do not know who is it," - admitted frankly Los.

Alexander, addressing to me, stood up for the visitors:

– "They have – absolutely another way of life. No reason to ask about it."

– "But we have to check them up somehow," - objected I. I looked at the icon of Christ standing on a shelf among books. That time it seemed to me that Christ should be the Lord for inhabitants of all planets in our Universe. Having shown the icon to aliens, I asked: - "How do you like this picture?" – I decided not to ask directly – "Who is he?", and if he was familiar to them then they should recognize him.

– "Yes, it is very interesting," - agreed Edar. – "it has good radiations."

The answer did not satisfy me, I needed to exact, therefore it was necessary to ask a direct question:

– "And do you know, who is on it?"

–"On it – there is a living being. But as we have not met him earlier, we do not know, whom you are talking about," - answered Edar.

– "But is there on your planet any spiritual leader?" - I continued to find out.

– "Yes, we have the Spirit, named Geyros. He is our teacher, and we are so positively disposed to him. Geyros is many thousand years older than we. He has a very experienced soul in comparison with ours, therefore he knows and remembers more. He gives us advices, and with his help we have achieved much in development."

– "Does Geyros symbolize the Holy Spirit on your planet?" - I asked, but they again did not understand.

Our naivety those years concerning a way of life of other beings was great. With the same success we could ask inhabitants of Guinea or the Hawaiian Islands whether they worship the portrait of our president. But through such clashes there was a perception of the world.

– "We do not know this Spirit," - answered Los. – "Geyros is the only one on our planet. But if it is necessary, we will make about him inquiries?" – It was obviously that the word "Holy" had been taken for a name. But I did not clear it up feeling that there was a clash in concepts. They had no religion, but there were respect and honoring of seniors. There was something similar in upbringing.

– "And is your Holy Spirit from «the Union of Spirits»?" – Los showed an interest.

– "Yes, probably, he is from the "the Union"," - I had to agree with him. It was necessary to find common ground between those idealistic images which they and we worshipped. Although his answer cleared up that they had another Higher Personalities to worship. Besides, the man was always sure that the one he/she worshiped, should be worshiped also by the others.

Seeing that their answer did not satisfy us for some reasons, Edar offered:

– "Allow us making inquiries about him. Do not you mind? There are many Higher souls in «the Union of Spirits». We do not know everybody. We are familiar only with the one who is attached to our planet."

– "If you have free time, then inquire," - Alexander agreed and asked with an interest: - "So you haven't your own home right now, all has been destroyed, have you?"

– "No, it remains in the past. Our houses were rebuilt long time ago, we have place where to live," - answered Los. – "But we left the planet long ago, and are in the flight for a long time. We have visited five planets before your Earth, and worked everywhere. As for our planet it is peace for the present.

Edar added:

– "I got to myself a new musical instrument and compose much. Los and I have an excellent ear for music, therefore the music of your colleague (for some reason he called this word Larisa) attracted us."

– " Are you the composer?" – Larisa asked.

– "I do not know this word," - admitted Edar. – " What does it mean?"

– "This is a person who composes new melodies, songs," - explained the daughter.

– "Yes, yes, I am a composer," - joyfully took up Edar and, came closer to the daughter, carefully touched her long fluffy hair, admitting: - "I like white color. And I, unfortunately, - dark. You know, long hair is aerials. They help to adjust communication with the Space, with your Teacher."

– "Therefore, likely, the majority of earthly composers prefer to have long hair," - Larisa noticed and addressed to Edar: - "However, what do you compose: melodies, songs or any big works, like symphonies?"

– "Everything what comes to mind. But basically – songs. I make up words by myself too," - confessed Edar.

– "And could you compose something clear for us?"

– "Certainly. We flew recently by the planet Mars, and I liked it. Then I made up something at once. In your language it will sound as follows:

The life on Mars is so good,
The man can find light and warmth,
If I could follow the crowd, I could,
But distant planet calls and draws.
We shall be flying lots of time,
Achieving purpose, study, work.
Such beings you will never find,
And who will find, will be shocked.

But in our images I compose, certainly, better, but yours I have not absolutely learned yet. I have not enough earthly concepts. Is it possible to get the additional information here?" – He addressed to Larisa.

– "Please. All our information is here, in books." - the daughter came to set of furniture where there were directories, scientific, esoteric literature on the shelf. – "But how will you read if you do not know our alphabet?"

– "We can perceive through energetics of words. If to read by means of letters you, likely, know that each letter bears its own energy, and some of them together form the energy of an image. Perceiving this energetics, we acquire also your concepts. But we are capable of various types of perception, there are several ways. We use the one which is proper for a concrete situation," - explained Edar and began to view books, and I addressed Los.

– "You are, as beings, made of less dense matter, than we. Does it mean that the force of gravity is less on your planet, than on the Earth?"

– "Yes, it is very small. In two hundred times is less regarding your matter, and as to ours – it is less. Regarding us the gravity force has a certain value. If we throw upwards a stone, it will never come back. And on the Earth it falls immediately."

– "So how do you move on the planet? – asked Larisa.

– "Our way of moving is more perfect: sometimes we go, like you and sometimes we fly, i.e. do enormous jumps, in your case. We can freely hang up in the air. And can you?" – One could find some complacency in Los's intonation. The way a child boasts of when he/she surpasses in something the other one. Los obviously felt the superiority in the ways of moving.

– "No, we do not move in the air without flying machines," - with some regret said the daughter. – "but there are separate people who possess a big energy and with the help of it are able to levitate in the air. However, it is very difficult. Ordinary people cannot do that."

Having diverted his attention from books for a moment, Edar entered into conversation:

– "If to take you on our planet, you could fly too, because the gravity force there is small. You would not go, but float in the air, without feeling a surface underfoot. This is a wonderful feeling, believe me!" – he spoke with admiration, like true romantic, so that we wished to fly together with him.

I speak - «with admiration» or with feeling of "complacency", catching such fine points of their intonation, because when the channeler translated someone's speech, he completely personified himself with this being and precisely transferred not only intonation of its speech, but even a mimicry. Therefore we clearly imagined, what things answers of our visitors were supplemented with, and how they perceive these or those questions or answers. This additional intonation and mimicry as though spiritualized dry answers which were depersonalized and ungenerous.

– "Then you enjoy movements, don't you?" – asked Larisa.

– "Yes. For me personally it is a pleasure," - confirmed Edar. – "I like to fly and compose verses about such beautiful beings as you," - he paid a compliment to the daughter, but she did not pay attention to it.

– "Can you only fly and hang up in the air ?" – She asked.

– "I can do different exercises in the air. Others like it. It comes out very well," - boasted he.

– "You are, likely, the gymnast in our language, are you?" – assumed the daughter.

– "Your language, it is possible so," - Edar agreed, but said: - "I am an aerialist."

– "How do you move on the Earth? Is it necessary for you to lean on a firm surface, to spring from it, to move ahead in the necessary direction? The man, for example, should necessarily have firm soil underfoot."

– "We are capable to move in every direction: forward, back upwards, downwards. The gravity force does not influence us so much. No surface for pushing away is necessary for us. We can freely go at level of your table or a ceiling. But not to shake human imagination by unusual for him/her ways of movement, we try, when you see us, to move like you."

– "People can swim in the water just as you in the air," - Larisa tried to show possibilities of the man and, having stopped her sight at the artificial flowers standing in a vase on one of shelves of a set of furniture, showed an interest asking: - "And do flowers grow on a planet?"

– "We have little vegetation, and no flowers at all. There are another plants there. They have another structure. Your plants please the eye, and ours – the ear. They are able to sound."

– "Surprisingly! We have never heard about such things," - eyes of the daughter lighted up with sincere admiration. – "Such plants, likely, help to compose music."

– "Why do you have not enough plants?" – I asked with an interest. – "Don't you plant them or the climate does not make it possible on the planet?"

– "We tried to bring flowers from other planets, but they do not strike roots because of sharp temperature changes," - Los answered. – "Precipitation happen in the form of rain, but they can be very cold because our liquid is not water, but compound similar to it, and it has temperature much more low, than water. For earthly, for example, plants it is hard. On the other hand our winds are weaker, than on the Earth. Hurricanes never happen. However some time ago they got us down, but we put energetical protection. It rescues us."

Edar, continuing his examination of books, suddenly came off a book shelf and addressed to Larisa:

– "This book is about some sort of yoga. What is it?"

– " This is a technique of exercises for a physical body, and yogis – people who are engaged in the given exercises," - explained the daughter and in her turn addressed to him the question: - "And do you know, that many beings besides a visible body have also subtle ones?"

– "Of course. We know everything," - Edar nodded with a dignity.

– "And what do you know about the man that is not present in our books?" – The daughter tried to find out some secrets about human structure, unknown to us, but the Edar's answer disappointed her. However, a bit unusual aliens' perception of earthly dwellers revealed in the answer.

– "Your books are about adventures, some fantasy, philosophy," - he started his speech. – "but in these books I found nothing about the most important thing: that the person is a rational being. And his brain is filled with different problems. He lives, studies. And about his mind nothing is written here. How does it work? Perhaps I have not found this book? Have you it? It is the most important thing."

– "There was such a book. I will bring it now," - replied Alexander and went to another room. A minute later he brought a big thick book «the Brain, Mind and Behavior», telling just about functioning of a human brain. Having put it on the table, he offered: - "Please examine. It seems to me, it is what you are looking for. Should I open it for you or leave it closed? How are you going to read it?"

– "Remain it closed, please. We can read it in any position. Closed or opened, there is no difference for us. We have such vision – we see through the cover and through other pages. Also we read, without turning the pages," - answered Edar.

– "We have a lot of books where numbers and formulas are written. Are such books clear to you or do they mean nothing for you?" – I asked.

– "We love formulas very much," - confessed Edar. – "We calculate with them what will turn out. This is – energy, too. Numbers contain more energy, than letters. If one formula add to another, new energy will come out. Los and I like to do such calculations. This is a very interesting occupation.

– "People call it mathematics," - informed Alexander.

– "Of course, we call it another way. And calculation methods – differ. I saw a book at your colleague (this word he called Larisa again) with numbers. But our calculations go within other schemes. It is connected with our matter. Your formulas are calculated on your matter, and ours – on ours."

– "But besides mathematical formulas we have also physical and chemical formulas, calculations. And do you have one more else specialization?" - asked I with an interest.

– "We have even more, but cannot translate them into your language, because it does not contain our concepts."

– "And how quickly do you read?" – Larisa was interested in. – "for example, this book," - she pointed out to the book which had been brought by Alexander, - "the man will read for a month. And how much time will it take for you?"

– "For us twenty minutes are enough."

– "For the person it is very quickly," - the daughter was surprised. – "if people had read with such a speed, everybody would have been superclever."

– "We do not need speed in reading. We read through concepts, we have our own technique."

Los interfered.

– "Do you consider: twenty minutes it is quickly? And for us it is very slowly. You think in vain that it is quickly. The fastest reading is three-five minutes."

– "We compare with the person," - explained I.

– "O-oh, clearly," - drawled he. – "yes, we have noticed that the person is a slowed-down being."

– "Yes, we have slowed-down reactions," - agreed Alexander.

– "We have noticed, you build buildings also for a long time," - again spoke Los. – "But we can construct the house in your terms for one day."

– "It takes one year for us to build a five-floor house," - confirmed Alexander. – "How do you manage to erect a building so quickly?"

– "We use special techniques and material. First we fill a mass in the ready form, and it stiffens when we switch on certain impulses. We have strict discipline, everyone accurately performs his/her work, therefore building goes quickly."

– "And do you take into consideration somehow in your constructions a small gravity force?" - Alexander was interested. He was a constructing-engineer, projected buildings and constructions, therefore he was interested in this issue purely from the professional point of view."

– "Yes, we use special fastenings." – answered Los. – "As the gravity force is rather small, then our houses are in addition fastened to the planet with strong ties. If all additional measures are not taken, our buildings can collapse and fly to atmosphere."

We noticed that from two aliens everyone specialized in certain themes: Los answered questions of the general character, and Edar as a humanist, preferred to speak about books, music. And his romantic appearance fully corresponded to it.

– "How do you breathe on the Earth?" – asked I. – "The atmosphere on your planet and ours is different. Do you use any appliances?"

– "The parallel world of your planet is similar to our world. We normally endure your atmosphere. However, recently we have visited your special territories near stations, the air there is very bad. We wonder, what do people breathe near them? Even for us to be in these radiations was hard. The air is very dirty. We see such places on a planet as dark areas. And the planet itself, where these stations are located, is dirty, too. In such places we turn on a special device – a cleaner. It creates round us a protective field and produces inside air, which is required for breath."

– "Is your planet clean everywhere?"

– "Yes. We maintain order. It is very clean there, nobody allows such pollution, as on your Earth. We are shocked, how your Spiritual Councils allow it. Don't they really see what your stations do?" - (I understood that Los called factories as stations.) – "All your nature is very dirty. We observed many times: everywhere in dwelling zones there are the dust, some wastes. Everything is shedloads, everything is in disorder. And the air is too bad. It is not clear to us, how are you still alive? Likely, your beings do not live long life, do they?"

– "Length of human life now is sixty-seventy years," - answered I.

– "Certainly, our time is another and it is difficult to compare, but I feel that you live for some instants."

– "And what is your length of life?" - I asked with an interest.

– "On our planet the average life length if to speak in your measure units, fluctuates from eighteen thirty two *(1832*-translator's notes)* years to forty five thirty three *(4533*-translator's notes)* years." – he for some reason said to an approximation of one year, although it would be possible to round off to ten years, but, probably, accuracy was rather significant for our understanding.

– "What are the reasons of death?"

– "What do you want to ask under "reasons"?" – did not understand Los.

I explained:

– "The man dies because of a serious illness, in accident, other people can kill him."

– "We have no murders at all. How is it so - to kill the same, as you?" – Los was obviously amazed. – "It is wildness indeed. Does it really happen here?"

– "Yes, there are lots of such cases here. In wars people kill each other, and without wars."

– "Then you, if to take Spirit development, stand very lowly in comparison with us. Higher beings do not kill each other already. Our wars show up only in destructions and temporary neutralization of beings or their capture. Our wars are waged in another way."

– "If you are such higher, you could do without destructions," – Alexander said as a man offended for a human race by that he had been ranked among low level civilizations.

– "You see, we do destructions," – Los began to explain mildly. – "to deprive them of their planetary level values. Everything what is constructed of a planet matter, refers to planetary values, but things which help to develop our Spirit refer to spiritual wealth."

– "Yes, people have the same division," - confirmed Alexander.

– "When someone has less planetary values," - continued an explanation Los, - "it becomes dependent on us. But, on the other hand, they begin to develop spiritually faster and more qualitatively. Wars here facilitate development of everyone's Spirit. There is a rethinking of the existence."

– "Why do you capture beings? Isn't it low, too?" – doubted my husband.

– "It is favourable for us to take prisoner because, the more beings we have, the more powerful we become."

– "But what do you do with your captives? Do you deal hardly with them?"

– "Never. They only change a usual way of life. It after all also makes inconveniences for Spirit. They should get used to all new, study something. Inconvenience for them consists in that desires of the captured are not taken into consideration. They, for example, wish to study one thing, but we need a worker in other field, and we teach him that."

– "What helps your beings to live so long: a correct way of life or something else?"

– "Our beings are kindly disposed to each other, unlike yours. We have noticed that people are very aggressive in relations with each other. But we look after the health of everyone; we help each other, and everybody – as one big, on the whole planet, family. We have such relations. As we have understood, a human health is influenced badly by temptations. They shorten life. We do not have temptations, therefore we develop faster and live longer."

– "Do you use for health strengthening any special exercises?" – My husband tried to find out. – "Perhaps, are there such techniques which help to get better?"

– "Yes, we constantly are engaged in special exercises, how is it called in your language..." - he was looking for a suitable word.

– "... sports," - suggested Alexander.

– "Yes. But our exercises differ from yours. They consist in concentration of energy, operation of it. By means of exercises our body receives a big inflow of energy which sustains life of beings ..."

– "... life-support," – suggested once again Alexander.

Los agreed by having nodded and continued:

– "There are cleaners at our stations. We conduct the right way of life – and all together contribute to our longevity. If the person learns to dispose correctly his life, he/she will be also allowed to live long. Understand please – short lives are because of human incorrect disposal of the life. He/she spends it for pleasures or dawdling, although it is necessary to spend it for development."

While Alexander and Los were discussing problems of the general character, Edar continued to study our books. I came to the daughter and whispered:

– "Let's try to invite them to have supper. Go and prepare something please, you may boil macaroni as it was faster. Tomato sauce is in a refrigerator. Salad, please make vegetable, cut fruit."

The daughter went to the kitchen, but was alone not for a long time. Seeing that Larisa disappeared, Edar lost his interest to books in one moment and went behind her.

Dmitry, having easily translating explanations of Los, suddenly began to worry and ceased to listen to him.

– "Why have they retired? I see through a wall that Edar is standing near Larisa. No, I cannot translate so. He is whispering something to her ear. Let's go, I will translate. She will not understand him."

Certainly, the young man did not care about Los, he did not want to stay Edar and Larisa alone, therefore went after them. Everybody had to move to the kitchen.

– "We wish to show the visitors our cooking," - I informed the daughter who at the moment was putting macaroni into the boiling water and stirring slowly with a spoon to prevent them from sticking together.

– "Edar asks you, what are you doing here?" – Began to translate Dmitry.

She became confused for a moment, thinking, how to explain visitors her actions, and then found a necessary explanation.

– "Our material body demands constant feed, therefore we have to prepare specially for it an additional material," - explained the daughter.

The explanation somehow did not precisely find expression in the sense of happening. And it was for the first time when we faced the fact how difficult it was to translate usual for us actions, which we got used not to think about, into another concepts.

– "How can we explain it more clearly to them?" - it flashed in my brain. I felt that they did not understand the heard. – «What do we cook food for?». But Larisa understood sense of the action herself. Seeing that her words remained absolutely incomprehensible for visitors, she continued to develop the thought.

– "Our body needs material components. If we do not eat something for one day, our power will be exhausted, we begin to work badly, and will be languid."

– "You are recharged by energy!" – Edar joyfully exclaimed. The concept "energy" became a link between our world and theirs. – "We like to be recharged by energy too. It means, you specially first prepare it, and then are recharged, aren't you?"

– "Yes, we use energy only of a definite quality," – quickly passed to their level of concepts the daughter. – "our material body demands energy of strictly definite quality. We take energy out of vegetables, fruit, special products. But we cook them beforehand; we select special qualitative structure of energy. You use more subtle energy, and we eat more rough material one."

Last phrase, however, with a word "rough" they interpreted in their own way.

– "Rough energy! Does it mean, you belong to the dark?"

– "Not a bit of it! We consider ourselves light," - objected Larisa. – "we love good and we do not bear, when one beings offend the others."

It is necessary to note, that first time they and we always caught each other who what System of Space belonged to, i.e. to plus or minus one, and both had to convince the other side they were light.

Being satisfied with an assurance that we hurt nobody, Edar continued to ask with an interest questions about our food.

– "Where do you take vegetables, fruit?"

– "People grow them."

– "In your place (he means a city) near one dwelling we saw a big heap of small subjects. These were, likely, your vegetables brought for food?" – Curiously asked the alien, meaning a heap of the gravel unloaded near someone's house.

I couldn't help laughing, but I tried to control myself not to offend visitors. The matter was that Edar asked a question with the big importance, being sure that he did a correct assumption and considering himself in this plan far-sighted. The face of my husband flashed with a good-natured smile. The perception of the alien looked amusing, so we had to make some corrections.

– "No, these were not vegetables, but a heap of artificial stones," - explained Alexander. – "They are not used as food and they are not cooked, but we use them for building of constructions. Likely, someone is going to make an extension to the house. We cook other things."

I opened a refrigerator, got tomatoes, cucumbers, cheese and, having laid out on the table, explained:

– "These subjects here are considered edible for the man. They first should be washed, and then one may prepare a salad of them."

Explaining, I began to wash vegetables and to make supper. Visitors with an interest were observing our actions, making comments:

– "So much time for preparation."

– "Yes," - I agreed, - "it takes almost half of your life for cooking, moreover so much is required to earn money for its acquisition. Others grow up products, and we buy them."

– "It is a very long process of preparation," - repeated Los a bit disappointedly. – "Our recharge with energy occurs easier. We do not only recharge the ships with energy of stars, but also personal bodies too. You, likely, know that stars radiate different types of energy. For ship power we catch energy of one type, and for ourselves – another. It is very simple. You could be recharged by energy of your star, too. It has a rich spectrum."

– "We are partially recharged," - confirmed Larisa. – "Many people like to sunbathe and with a sunburn acquire certain types of energy, too. But it's not enough for the man. Our body is constructed in such a way that demands a set of different additional components. Do you use on your planet different types of energy?"

– "You have guessed," – Los nodded. – "energy from our star we use for different purposes: one is applied in building, another – for our machines, the third – for life of beings."

– "And what does the energy which is consumed by living beings represent?" – The daughter showed an interest.

– "How can I explain you …" - Los became confused. – "It is very tasty for us. By quality and type it corresponds to our external body. It is impossible to be recharged by any energy, otherwise you may destroy yourself. We have special small devices with a help of which we catch energy of the necessary type from a star and then direct it to ourselves. We enjoy it very much. For us additional charge by energy is a short instant."

While mentioning about the process of their food, a knife cutting a cucumber, stopped in my hands, and it flashed in a head: «Well, entertained aliens to supper. They, probably, have not stomach something to digest. With such food and the stomach is not necessary». But I admitted aloud:

– "We wished you to treat earthly food, but now we do not know, how to do it. You are recharged absolutely in another way."

Los understood our confusion and, not wishing to disappoint, calmed down:

– "However, we shall try your food, in our own way."

– "From hands of your colleague everything will be very tasty," - added Edar. (He continued to name Larisa the colleague. The reason of it was that all of them on the ship were colleagues in relations to each other. And he considered members of our family also colleagues.)

– "How will you eat?" – asked I with an interest.

– "Your food in our plane produces definite radiations. Vegetables have subtle covers, we see them. So from these covers we shall take for ourselves the energy which suits us more. We are capable to catch even aroma of your food."

A solemn supper, as we would like to have, did not come out. Frankly speaking, we showed, how in best traditions people do it. Beautifully laid the table, instead of a bunch of flowers in the middle of it we put a vase with a sprawling branch of a tree on which small color bulbs intended for a meeting of new year hung. Tape recorder was turned on. We sat down at the table four of us together with Dmitry, but two chairs left for Los and Edar. We put plates with their portions in front of them.

It was very amusing to have supper with invisible visitors. In some minutes, however, they informed that energy of our food was pleasant, and it was very beautiful at the table. They hadn't felt so well for a long time, because our small collective radiated kind emanations.

Our feast if to regard it in a detached spirit, could be possibly named – «supper of madmen». All the present by turns talked to empty chairs, addressing them as to the animated. But, strangely enough, it seemed to us that we saw their slight, as smoke, silhouettes.

We were eating. They observed us. The method of ingestion looked for them, obviously, strange because Edar did not sustain and commented:

– "Your energy recharge is very long, too. Your products require long preparation. First they are grown up, then you boil them, and then finish in yourself just for a long time. Many power and time are expended."

– "Yes, we understand it. But on the other hand we cannot," - agreed I.

– "We have momentary filling up. We have understood, why people have lagged behind us in development: instead of spending time for study, they spend all the day long for meal," -drawn a conclusion Los.

– "You are right," - Alexander agreed. – "However, the man, unfortunately, does not understand it. But we will tell people your remarks," - he joked.

Aliens took his statement seriously.

– "Yes, tell them our remarks. And we also would like them not to meet other beings in such malicious and spiteful way."

– "Well. We will tell," - I confirmed and addressed to Edar: - "Have you read our books on theosophy? Is there something wrong from your point of view?"

– "All beings reflect concepts close to them in their own way. We have data storehouses, too. However, it consists not in books, but in special recordings."

– "Diskettes," - supposed Alexander.

– "We cannot judge correctness of your information because you know one things, and we – another, although some discrepancy we catch," - Edar declared. – "you see your dimention, and we – ours. Who of us can be right? If you tell that our ship does not exist, we shall tell that it does. You will be right for your world and for beings with the same level of perception, as you. And we shall be right for our world."

– "And do you know much about numbers? What does interrelation exist between number and energy?" – I tried to find out.

– "Energy is divided into numbers," - Los entered the conversation. – "They let us define, how much energy goes to this or that side. But we cannot explain you it because you do not have such concepts."

– "We know that every person has the code. What can you tell us about a code?"

–"The general code of the person – 9935 units. It is his exchange with the Space, some average indicator. An individual code of the man tells – how much energy his/her organism processes per one year. How much energy increases and decreases in total. There is a circulation of this energy. And everything is calculated. Would you like, we shall give you the technique how to calculate your own energy?" – offered Los.

– "What will this figure give to us? What advantage shall we have?" – Alexander wasn't delighted with such a knowledge.

– "You will know your energetical level per year. Isn't it really interesting to you?"

– "Interesting."

– "If you produce less, than you need, in this case you will have problems in destiny."

– "And what should we do to increase the productivity?"

– "To rise the development level and to purify energetic channels. We know that the higher a being in development, the more energy it is capable to produce for the Space."

– "Why increase? Is not it enough for us? I do not notice this energy produced by me at all," - my husband, remaining indifferent to production of own energy, objected.

– "You do not notice, but Spirits, who supervise you, notice all. Haven't you thought, that if you begin to occupy nothing, energy will flow to you? No, it won't, it will decrease. It is necessary to study constantly and clear the channels. We share the knowledge with you, because we passed the same stage of development, as you, long time ago. The most important thing for every being, whatever world it lives in, is to increase the power. Have not you known about it?"

– "No," - frankly admitted Alexander. – "We hear it for the first time."

– "You have well received us, that is why we tell," - confidentially informed Los. – "We give you this information as to our new friends. May we call you this way?"

– "Sure," - almost in chorus we answered, and I added: - "We are glad that we have such friends, and we can learn something about each other."

– "And how much time in earthly chronology to fly from the Earth to your planet?" - Larisa addressed to Edar.

– "If to consider that we are in other dimension and we have another time units and speeds, for half a year it is possible to reach. The ship moves with high speed, the man cannot imagine it."

– "Do you have a division by professions? You fly, and there should be doctors, technicians on the ship. On your planet someone built this ship. Are there other professions?" - asked I.

– "And how do you think? Of course, are. There are both doctors, and builders, who build premises for other beings, constructors, and many other occupations on the planet. We do not know, how to translate you them."

– "Who is engaged in technics, that refers to technical workers," - I supposed. – "who composes the music, that is musician. By the way, do they sing in chorus?" – just for fun I asked.

– "What is it?" – Edar didn't understand at first.

– "It is when many beings sing one song," – my husband explained.

– "There sings only the one."

– "Please suggest several your beings to sing together. You will become a discoverer," - he offered Edar. – "You will invent a new genre."

– "No, it will not turn out to sing together there. A lot of energy is given off during a singing of one being. And if many beings sing, they will break power protection of the planet. This is impossible for us."

– "Well, then you will bring our earthly songs to the planet," - Larisa offered him. – "I will teach you."

– "I will necessarily bring. I like your melodies very much. May I ask you to play once again," - he addressed to the daughter. – "I will remember melodies."

Larisa agreed, and visitors immersed in sounds of earthly music again. Edar became sad. His big eyes were filled with grief. Los had small eyes, therefore they did not so brightly express his feelings, but nevertheless the round face changed a good nature mask to a mask of severe thoughtfulness. It said about that for their long lives they saw a lot of unpleasant and, moreover, sad. Therefore, when Larisa stopped to play, I asked with an interest:

– "You live long in comparison with people, do you remember everything from the past or much is forgotten, like the human?"

– "We do not know what the human forgets," - Edar told, - "but we remember everything, every day. Our memory volume is very big."

– "And it does not prevent to live, does it?"

– "No, we remember selectively, only what is necessary for business or for feelings. Now I am listening to your music and remember to play it then by myself. I have rather good memory for music."

– "How much time will you stay on the Earth?"

– "Half a year in your way of calculation. We have to study much here, to carry out experiments and to get some schemes for devices."

– "Are you interested only in devices?" – I asked, noting that it was of great significance for them.

– "Not only in them. We are interested in terrestrial nature, environment, and atmosphere. We wish to learn more about people. We are glad that have found here the person who understands us. It will allow to learn people better. When you regard them in a detached spirit, it will be of no use. But such close communication reveals much that we would never have learned from the outside."

At this moment somebody tooted the ringer, and I went to open. Michael Fadeev and Vladimir Gromov entered the vestibule. They were members of our club investigating abnormal phenomena. Michael for that period was thirty years old, and Gromov – forty two. But despite the age difference, they were friends and often read together esoteric books aloud, discussing pleasant passages. They often took our books to read. That time they came to return a read book.

– "We return in its entirety and good condition," - Michael held me out «Rose of the World» by Andreev (*Andreev* * - *last name of the writer, translator's note*). – "Did something new appear?"

– "Not so far," - I gave a short answer hurrying up to return to visitors.

But Michael was not going to leave quickly.

– "What are you doing?" – He was curious, seeing that we did not invite them to move along for some reason as usual. I had to admit that we had visitors.

– "Sorry. I cannot invite. Dmitry has a contact with aliens from Sirius. We have two newcomers from the subtle world. You are not acquainted with them; we need first beg them permission."

Mr. Gromov had abilities to clairvoyance. He could not hear beings from other worlds, but with a certain tuning could see them. Having pried, he concentrated and, muttered: «Now we shall check», began to observe the room.

– "O-o," - he joyfully drawled, - "Indeed. But how haughty they are. They are looking askew at us, thinking, they are under the shelter." – he was a self-confident man and by no means delicate, therefore concluded right away: - "Not handsome men, but resemble us. Especially that, bald, resembles me very much. Well, in so many words – like I. I only have ten hairs more on a head," - he joked. – "and the burning brunette is near. I see such for the first time."

He precisely enough deduced likeness of Los and himself. I had not thought of it somehow, but when he told that one of aliens was similar to him I fully agreed. Vladimir Gromov was full-blown, tonsured, but as for height, maybe, a bit higher than Los.

– "I am not against to communicate with them," - he expressed his desire.

– "Me, too," - consented to friend Michael.

– "Not today. We need to arrange with them first. Agree or not, nobody knows. Right now – sorry," - I made a hint that it was time to say goodbye.

– "Well. We are waiting for a meeting. Try to agree, please," - whispered Michael.

They left, and I came back to the room. Having taken my former seat at the table, I passed at once to negotiations.

– "Two our companions have just come to us. They would like to have a talk with you. Are you not against?"

– "We have heard how they badly responded about us – «not handsome, bald»," - with insult in the tone said sensitive Edar. – "If they were not into us, so then what for should we meet? It is not clear for me. And is «burning brunette» something negative?"

– "Please, excuse them. They are simply kidding. They are good people, but in conversation they take some liberties. And «the burning brunette» is a very positive name."

– "We know that many people do not believe in us, from their point of view, we do not exist at all. It is offensive. And we do not wish to meet such non-believers."

– "There are other people in our club, they believe. They are interested in everything," – assured I. "But they come short of communication culture. It happens very seldom when they meet such interesting beings, as you. But good manner should be studied, experience is necessary," - I tried to persuade them.

– "All right, we will think and then we will inform you," – edulcorated Los. – "And now it is high time for us. Pleasant recharge," - he wished just in his manner and then added in an earthly way: -"As people say, see you soon."

– "All the best to you, too. Good luck," – wished we.

When they left, Dmitry with appetite waded his portion, which remained on the table untouched. He translated, and there was no time to eat.

Larisa, imitating aliens, playfully wished him:

– "Pleasant recharge."

– "Yes, I am pinched with hunger. If you only know, how ridiculously they tasted our food. They as though inhaled steam from it. Los mostly inhaled macaroni. Probably, he enjoyed them more, and Edar tasted tomatoes in a salad."

– "Well, that means, they have tasted our terrestrial food," - Alexander said with satisfaction. – "I was afraid that they wouldn't taste it. At least evaporations let them have an idea about it."

– "As for us we will not feel their energy, as we have such a rough matter," - said disappointedly Larisa. – "we are lack of the fifth dimension."

– "It is good to be invisible – they hang around apartments and nobody sees them," - with a full mouth muttered Dmitry and, having chewed, added: - "But it is bad for us. They keep watch over us, and we do not know."

– "Are you excited by their opinion?" – smiled Larisa.

– "No, not opinion. I have thought that," - and his eyes became round from concern. – "when someone bathes in a bathroom, they can peep. They are curious in everything: how we look like, and how we bathe." – he meaningfully looked at Larisa.

I understood that jealousy aroused in him, and he hinted that someone could pry about her, therefore I tried to calm him.

– "Do not worry. Before taking a shower we will check apartment with bioframes."

– "I do not trust bioframes," - disdainfully gave a wave of the hand Dmitry, - "they react to everything: any TV or radio set will take for a being."

– "You think so in vain. Biolocation works correctly. It has already been thousand times checked by me," - assured Alexander.

– "I offer, when Larisa is going to bathe, call me to check rooms. I will check apartment in advance with the third eye," - offered Dmitry.

The daughter laughed.

– "You see through walls. For you a bathroom is an open premise. No, no, no, I do not need such services. I trust daddy's frame more. He will check. And then, Edar and Los are not so as our curious men. They are higher beings. And the higher are not engaged in any meanness. Spying, eavesdropping are inherent in the low."

– "And we do not know still, higher they or low. If they fly on "plates" it does not mean that they have spiritually surpassed us," - the young man hotly objected. – "but as you wish. My job is to warn."

However, Dmitry's thought that invisible beings can keep watch over the man, seemed to us quite real. And we before bathing began really to check our apartment. Basically, it was empty. But one day, when the daughter was going to bathe, and was filling a bath with water, we really found out five strange fields in one of the rooms. Three of them made comfortable on a sofa, one took up a chair and another filled an armchair.

A suspicion crept into my mind: «Are there really our acquaintances»? I decided to check them up with a sign of the cross. But first tried to touch, i.e. to perceive their field with a palm.

A hand refers to rather sensitive parts of the body, it feels strange fields very much. That was why I hold out a hand to an armchair and began slowly locate air over it. I felt a slight pricking of invisible needles. Then move a hand aside from an armchair, in empty space to compare sensations in different places and at once felt a difference. Pricking disappeared. The difference in temperature was not felt. I placed a palm over an armchair. There was again a feeling of slight pricking. Having shifted to a chair, I repeated the actions. Here the pricking was felt more accurately.

The spouse made checks with the frame. It was found out that the field on a chair exceeded in radius the field in an armchair.

– "Someone more powerful is sitting here," - made a conclusion Alexander.

– "I do not think that these are our acquaintances," - began to protect aliens the daughter. – "they will not come without a translator. Most likely these are souls of the dead. Two days ago outstanding accident happened on the road, some persons died. While they are not taken away Upwards, they can walk about here. Now that we lighten in the subtle world more than others, they have come to this light. However, we can help them nothing.

Having investigated fields with a palm and a frame, I passed to a sign of the cross, began to cross diligently. All fields made move and shifted. Two of them "have run away" to the corridor.

– "There now! They are not ours," - Larisa was delighted. – "our friends are not afraid of the cross. These are some low ones, who have come to nourish by our energy."

I once again made a sign of the cross in places of assumed beings, and the room was cleared. But idea struck me to check the bathroom. The bath was just filled with water. The crane closed.

When Alexander put the frame in a premise, it went round there, as a propeller.

– "Oho," - exclaimed he with amazement. – "What a concentration of fields. It seems to me, all our friends have moved here. Perhaps, it will be necessary to clean here also with a candle."

– "Yes, bath day is cancelled," – said Larisa. – "there are too many visitors."

But without Dmitry we did not find out what were these visitors from the subtle world who visited us that evening.

Chapter 3

Aliens' Love

There was a Saturday day. Alexander took drawings to work at home and finished them as the project was urgent, and the customer demanded to carry the work to completion in the nearest terms. I was preparing dinner in the kitchen.

Somebody tooted the ringer. Dmitry came. I opened scarcely a door when he right off the bat enthusiastically and with emotions half-whispering begun to chatter:

– "Where is Larisa? I am for hundred percent sure that Edar is sitting in her room and observing her. He won't outflank me. I precisely know – they are here."

Larisa came out of the room with a book in her hands and also in tone to him half-whispering said:

– "It seems to me, you are right. I also have felt that there is somebody in the room. But how do you know, that we have visitors?"

Dmitry changed the whisper to hardly distinguishable. His eyes were burning with excitation. But I could not understand what had made him so excited, before he told.

– "I have seen such a thing! I am going to you and think: «It would be necessary to look – whether our visitors are nearby». I activated my inner sight on the street and the seen stopped me short of falling. I even stumbled upon an aunt, going towards me. She thought that I was drunk. But I saw such for the first time – there was a huge ship hanging over the roof of your house: lengthways was almost like this house and from top to bottom – four floors would be. But so beautiful. All was in some gimmickries, details, windows – in two rows. I even gasped. And people around me, were as blind kittens: went, too, and saw nothing. Nobody to compare notes. I, of course, - hurried to you … One minute, please, – I will check now …" - he activated the third eye and soon also in a whisper discontentedly said: - "Well, there now. No doubt, both of them are here."

Edar from the daughter's room got through two walls and kitchen to the hall where Alexander was drawing and where there was already Los near his drawing board.

– "If visitors have arrived, let's go and talk," - I offered Dmitry. – "Maybe, they are just waiting for you."

We came to a family room, and Dmitry on the fly began to translate the greeting of Los.

– "Bright star to you, kind deals," - aliens quickly adopted our etiquette, i.e. they knew that when people met they should tell a greeting, and when left – say goodbye. (They had other greetings). – "We have been standing here for a long time and keep watch, how you are working. What are you drawing here?" – Los addressed to my spouse.

– "It is a drawing of the residential house foundation,"-explained Alexander.

– "What is the foundation?" – asked again Los.

– "It is a bottom part of a building, it is located in the ground."

– "Do you draw the scheme and then build?"

– "Yes. And how is it on your planet?" – Alexander purely professionally asked with an interest.

– "We at first calculate, then we create holograms of premises, and then we build. We create everything on the basis of holograms. It is very convenient. But we have seen that there are many bad houses here and have understood that you do not have enough dwellings, and people take shelter in special premises made of tree. (this way aliens responded about wooden houses). It is tightly and dirty. We could not live that way. They live very badly."

They were talking about private houses which seemed to them unattractive. But we tried to explain it away.

– "These are temporary hardships. The time will come, and everybody will live in good apartments. And do you have big rooms?"

– "It is roomily on our end, we have never such narrowness. It seems to us that some people here live very badly, but you conceal it."

– "We do not conceal. It is indeed," - Alexander had to confess. – "But difficulties are because of long building. If we had your technology of building we, everybody, would live in palaces."

– "But dwellings made of wood are short-lived. Do they really hold out for one human life?" – Edar was surprised. – "On our end it would be necessary to build thousand similar houses. We live long."

– "The man in comparison with you lives a short instant that is why it is quite enough for one life" - answered Alexander.

While they were arguing about our earthly constructions, I decided to locate their fields with a palm to compare with that we had received in our research of unknown fields a bit earlier. Having put out hands, I began to "feel" air space, trying to feel the slightest changes of environment, and soon clearly felt a difference between empty space and those places where our visitors were sitting.

The first what I felt was a concentration of a field. It was tough in comparison with usual emptiness and strenuously pricked a palm as if a lot of discharges ran between me and it. A usual environment was soft and without mini - discharges. Moreover, unexpectedly I felt that air temperature in places of aliens' bodies location was higher. Obvious heat was felt where there was Los. It was necessary to take a palm aside, and the hand felt a cool. Our friends appeared lukewarm.

Larisa, having understood, what I was busy with, began to investigate aliens too and later confirmed my observations.

Edar paid attention to our strange movements, asked with an interest:

– "What are you doing?"

– "We measure your energy," - I explained shortly our actions.

– "Are you catching something?" – He was surprised.

– "Yes, we feel you," - confirmed Larisa.

Edar was delighted and asked her:

– "Put out a hand." – She put a palm out to him. – The alien cautiously thrusted out his one towards her and placed it over her palm. – "Do you feel?"

– "Yes," – she answered. – "I feel a warm touch."

– "I am very glad. Now then sense better. I will change concentration of energy."

– "I feel – the temperature raises, and pricking became more rigid … She listened to sensations once again and added: - "I began to feel tension of the field. Oh-o, palms become hot."

Edar rejoiced:

– "Now you will always feel me, and know, when I come."

– "Yes. We have come into contact between two worlds through sensations," - pathetically, but with some irony said the daughter.

– "To come to Misses without their permission is discourteously," - jealously declared Dmitry and added discontentedly: - "And in general to touch them too is impossible. The only bridegroom has such permission."

– "Who is it this Spirit?" - Edar politely enquired about. – "Does he occupy a high position?"

– "It is not a Spirit, this is a person," - muttered Dmitry. – "he should become a husband of a girl …" – He drew the line with further explanation. He did not know, how to explain aliens, who a groom was, and whom he was in respect of a girl. Many rules and norms of etiquette emerged which were simply impossible to translate into other concepts. He scratched his head and decided to go in an explanation the shortest way. – "A bridegroom of the girl becomes her husband, and then they have children. Do you have children on your planet?"

– "Yes, certainly." - Edar hardly understood, how the bridegroom became the husband, but the concept "children" proved to be general, and he skillfully joined it with theirs. – "There could be many children. They are also at first small, and then become grownup."

– "Does it mean, that there are also pretty girls on your planet, too?" – Dmitry turned Edar's attention from a dugout to aliens-women, hinting that, probably, he had a girl-friend, and a host of children. But Edar puzzled him:

– "There are no girls on our planet. All the beings are identical."

– "Are you same-sex?" – Dmitry became wide-eyed because of surprise, but doubts still continued to harrow up his soul. – "and then how do children appear?"

– "Two beings merge in a single whole, in one combined mass. Thus they stop existence as personalities. One matter comes out which then breaks into other small beings."

– "Does it hurt?" – Dmitry looked a little perplexedly.

– "No."

– "Is reproduction for you the end of existence as personalities?" – Alexander began helping the channeler to find out subtleties of such a delicate issue.

– "Yes. But we first live life-time, gain experience, and then at the ebb of life children appear. We do not die as the man does. Our corporal weight is transformed into body of following beings, unlike your mass which falls to components. But as we live many years our abundance is less, than earthly men."

– "But do you know with whom it is necessary to merge at the moment of death or does it occur spontaneously?" - specified Alexander.

– "Parinibanna corresponds to the moment of pregnancy. A special age is needed for this when beings should leave our world."

– "But where is the second partner from? Is he appointed specially or at will?"

– "Partners find each other themselves, come together by characters. If there is no accord, nothing will result, there will be no merge. When the pair satisfies each other, everything works out fine. They combine for some time, go together everywhere, fly. Unification of their subtle fields happens. Then there comes the moment – they merge and perish. And other beings appeared from a combined mass."

– "Does it mean that the pair has any special feelings to each other?" – I showed an interest. – "Do you have feelings?"

– "Yes. We have mutual respect."

– "Children appear from the mass, and there are no parents," - I noticed. – "but who then brings them up?"

Further Edar made an explanation, which remained unclear for those present, although the general scheme became apparent.

– "Education goes itself. It originates on the basis of a special bioenergy received from partners, while joining it with a program. Beings, who merge, first of all let off special energy. It increases, joining with small beings, and manage them. In other words children receive entirely that information, which their parents have owned, and use it for development."

– "Do they use it for definite time, and then gain their experience?" – I continued to ask details.

– "Yes. They have a program. It manages them. But on the basis of the information received from parents they bring up themselves, they know, what it is necessary to strain after, what to study."

– "As I have understood, all knowledge, which parents get, passes to their children. Therefore do they appear with that level of concepts, which have been got by parents?"

– "Yes, right. That is the reason why a progress of beings happens in our world. Don't you really have such knowledge transfer?"

– "No, with people – it's another way. Personal knowledge of parents is not transferred at the moment of birth. However, it is transferred later during educational process through speech, through books. There are a lot of libraries where the knowledge of people is stored."

– "On our planet there are storehouses of the general knowledge, too," - noticed Edar. – "But there are no books in storehouses, only special places, in which knowledge is written down in microcircuits. It allows storing a great scope of information in small volumes. Besides, our storehouses are cleared of out-dated and unnecessary information over some periods of time."

– "How do you know, that this or that information is false? Maybe in the future it will be useful. It happens so often: everything which seems now false, in the future appears true."

– "Our souls are older than human; we know what is right and what is not. We have a perceptual unity of semantic concepts, and our souls feel at once, where they do not correspond to the future life. Our soul sees the truth."

– " Do you have special schools where children study?" – asked Larisa.

– "No. Our children chose the right way for themselves, they are concerned with self-education. They feel their programme fastidiously and follow it. As for you, we have noticed, that there are lots of so-called fools who lop about." – Edar's ton became censoriously severe. – "they gad about and cannot find any place, they want nothing to achieve if only drink potables from the dark and blow off gases, to poison others with them (this way the alien said about a smoke from cigarettes). Do you understand these words?"

Larisa agreed, having nodded.

– "That's right. We thought that aliens did not notice it."

– "Oh, don't say that!" – emotionally enough exclaimed Edar. – "This first of all strikes everybody's eye. These beings produce dark or red radiations. We are surprised, how many people on the Earth who give in to any temptations. It's not the deal to drink bad drinks and then lounging around somewhere illegally or to give in to the power of the dark.

– "People do not realize it," - said ruefully the daughter, and father added:

– "We consider that they spiritually have not grown up."

– "That's it," - agreed Edar and continued: - "They know nothing and nothing want to learn. It is better for them to think that we and other worlds do not exist. Do not you know, these are out-of-spec souls?"

– "No, we always consider that the man is the man, and it is necessary to struggle for him," - objected Larisa. It was unpleasant for her to listen about degrading people. – "Our society constantly tries to return them on a righteous way." – and wishing to switch gears, asked: - "Does it happen at your end, that someone does not find himself a partner? Then he can exist eternally." – she said the last phrase jocoseriously, understanding impossibility of the given assumption and therefore at once adjusted at once: - "Or does his end come in this case?"

– "This never happens. A partner is found definitely. The number of our beings is always even. But, let us say, two pairs of four have not come together. And then they swap over. They do not come together because of mental qualities, but as a result of the exchange grading takes place. At the beginning error occurs, then partners swap over and everything normalizes. The main thing which is taken into consideration in selection is those qualities which they have. Qualities and knowledge of one partner should supplement qualities and knowledge of other partner and then children appear miscellaneous, possessing great volume of knowledge necessary for them. Variants of pairs of four beings are as follows:" - and he gave the scheme, which is below:

$$A + B \qquad A + C \qquad A + D \qquad \text{variants of pairs}$$
$$D + C \qquad D + B \qquad D + A \qquad \text{of four beings.}$$

– "However, do among new beings, i.e. children result almost all healthy and normal? Do you have defective?" – asked Larisa again.

– "In rare cases it happens, but they are eliminated. You spend for your fools at first many resources in vain, and then they are cleaned up through death. And we clean up at the beginning and save means."

– "And do you know, what is pity, humanity?"

– "What do you mean? We are not familiar with them. Please, explain."

– "People feel sorry for each being. They try to help to settle down to a righteous course. They feel bad because of their low intellect, but they do not understand, how to improve the life. Thus cleverer people should help the silly."

I noticed that it was difficult for Larisa to transfer Edar ideas about humanity and good. And I myself felt the complexity of the offered explanation. Sometimes it is difficult to explain the concept of humanity even to the person, and to aliens all the more. But, strangely enough, visitors understood us better, than we them. Obviously, it was because of longer evolution of their souls having gained big experience.

– "We also have similar relations," - confirmed Edar. – "they are called, frankly speaking, in another way. Such good qualities in our beings are developed more, than in the man. But we select children more carefully. Therefore we have less defects, and simultaneously there is a saving of means. I am glad that your colleague is worried about existence of high qualities in people."

Edar came to the daughter and touched her hair as if they were stroked. It was a usual practice on their planet to reveal their favor in relation to someone.

Dmitry disliked the liberty of the visitor, he interpreted this gesture in his own way and discontentedly grumbled:

– "If you do not have the opposite sex, then why do you tack on earthly girls?"

– "Whataya, I do not tack," - Edar understood him literally. – "Look, we are divided by air."

– "And how are your children connected to an adult life?" – not paying attention to nagging of the young man, continued conversation the daughter. – "They are, likely, taught by adults?"

– "No, they do it themselves. They have an experience received from parents. They have all the necessary information from them. It helps to be guided correctly in life. But as far as children grow, their information increases, too, keeps up to date. Since childhood they think over the future, purposefully choose what they are more interested in, and develop in this direction."

While Edar was conducting a talk, Los did not utter a word and not even once interrupted. His silence quickened my interest, and I asked Dmitry:

– "What is Los doing right now? Why is he silent?"

In some seconds the young man mockingly informed:

– "He has saturated himself in your alarm clock. Nevertheless he has got it. He is examining gears. You have forgotten to hide it, now say it goodbye. Owse, how they like devices. They like nothing better than rummaging in it. May I tell him to stop?" – He addressed me.

But I waved my hand:

– "All right, let him break completely. Communication requires sacrificing."

But I worried in vain. Los, having studied all small screws and gears of alarm clock, did not break it so it continued to work normally further. Visitors caused no damage, and we began to trust them more.

An idea struck my mind - to introduce aliens to our group of enthusiasts. They were just people who were interested in everything unusual. Once a week they gathered in our apartment, everyone came with some new information, which was discussed, and then everybody exchanged opinions. Parallel to that we were conducting contacts to the Higher Space System, called "the Union". So there were double channelings: with aliens, who, let us consider, were similar to us, and with the System "the Union", which belonged to the Hierarchy of God.

The group, basically, was present during channelings of the Higher, but that moment there was a possibility to introduce them to equal ones. Therefore I addressed with the offer about a meeting to Los, considering him the senior although aliens and had not told us about it. But judging by seriousness of Los, I decided that he occupied among them a predominating position.

– "We have a group of people, which is interested in everything unusual and new. Would you mind to meet them?"

– "First of all we would like to know who are these personalities," - seriously said Los. – "Will they betray us? After all we are present here secretly from people. But we have heard that when people find out something about aliens, they start catch them at once and put in closed premises. We do not bear it. First we would like to know something about these persons, whether they will cause damage to us."

– "Do not worry, we guarantee safety of a meeting to you," - assured I. – "Nobody will give you out. Moreover, people are capable to catch only material beings. As for you, you are subtle-mattered, currently none of our devices will find out you. And besides, you easily go through any walls. Our scientists have not invented still such materials which could keep you in isolation. So you have nothing to be afraid of people."

– "Whatever happens," - replied Los. – "you cannot know what your high-ranking scientists have invented."

– "Do not worry. In any case people of our group have nothing in common with them. These scientists are far away from ordinary people."

I managed to persuade them to meet with the group. Day and time were appointed.

Members of our group with an interest took an offer to get acquainted with the aliens. Nobody responded with mistrust that they were invisible. Our people were already advanced in the knowledge of a subtle world so that a meeting with invisible beings was for them natural, as well as a meeting with common persons. They would be surprised more to meet with some foreigners, than with invisible beings. Therefore by appointed time members of group had begun to gather in our apartment.

First came Michael Fadeev and Vladimir Gromov. Gromov began to attend our group one year ago and as we were constantly in a zone of powerful energy his third eye activated, and he saw the beings, who were close to the etheric and astral plane. So it needs here to say, that every clairvoyant works in his own range of frequencies. One focuses the third eye on a physical matter, i.e. on a rough spectrum of frequencies, the eye of another one works in higher spectrum and consequently sees etheric and astral beings.

Clairvoyants working with a higher range energy, see other beings. Therefore, if to take three clairvoyants working with a different spectrum of energy frequencies, so being in one room, they will see different essences, because they will connect into different subtle worlds. And if, let us say, three clairvoyants give different results in one experiment it speaks about their different levels of development and different subtle construction, so they see different worlds.

Peculiarities of clairvoyance are explained by nuances of their subtle structures construction.

Next to pair of friends Nikolay Salkin with the wife, Molodtsova Natalia and some more persons came. As it turned out there were more people than I had invited, all the vacant seats were occupied. Hosts, namely me and Alexander, failed to take seats, and there were not spare chairs at home. Two chairs were intended for our space visitors – Los and Edar, therefore they remained free. Certainly, aliens did not need most likely our material chairs, but there was a work of our purely human habits and that was why we adapt for our conventionalities other beings.

Everybody took seats and waited, quietly talking over. Soon Dmitry informed:

– "They have come and taken seats. Los and Edar welcome those present." – and further the channeler started talking solemnly already on behalf of them, translating Los words: - "the Planet 327 welcomes Earthmen represented by you. The third parallel world gives you kind wishes. We meet with such a big community for the first time."

– "Our people are glad to get acquainted with representatives of other world. This is the first meeting for them, too, therefore they have come openheartedly and with light thoughts," - I greeted them on behalf of the present and addressed members of the group: – "Please, ask what you are interested in."

Vladimir Gromov addressed to them first.

– "How long will you be here and what purpose have you arrived for?"

– "For a long time, till we finish to study specific conditions. Our purpose is – examination of devices, concerning electronic modification," – answered Los.

Both aliens were sitting on chairs, but my husband and I stood near the table, because of lack of vacant seats.

– "Why are you interested in our equipment?" – asked with an interest Mr.Gromov.

– "For protection of our beings we need a device with the screen. But it is necessary not personally to us, but for those who govern us. We have got the task from them."

– "And have you found approximately such a device?" – asked Mr.Gromov.

– "Not yet. Approximately such a device as we were informed by other beings, should be in the latest model of your black box," - informed Los.

– "What is it «a black box»?" – Natalia Molodtsova did not understand.

– "Likely, the TV," - guessed at once Nikolay Salkin, who was a communications engineer working for radio manufacturing plant.

Los confirmed his assumption, having pointed out our TV set.

–"It is a device similar to yours. But this is outmoded, and we need new."

A wide soul of Russian person at once responded with kind wishes. Nikolay Salkin involved in TV manufacture, instantly graciously offered them:

– "Please, go to a radio manufacturing plant. There are enormous shops with the newest devices. Choose what fits you."

Natalia, working for the same plant as a designer, hospitably consented:

– "Yes, different marks, there is much to choose."

A noble Russian soul without any dissembled thought rushed at once to help others at first mentioning that someone required something. It is possible even to say that in some souls of our companions it has already turned to an instinct - to help the others on the first signal of asking for help, without thinking about consequences, without assuming that, probably, it can sometime turn back against them. But this is a Russian person – only hint that you need help, and he will lay him/herself out to help. Therefore and others began to advise.

– "You may look for in shops," - suggested Mr.Gromov.

– "And it is better at exhibitions," – said Mr.Fadeev. – "The newest equipment can be found there."

– "What is the exhibition?" – asked Los. The word "newest" quickened obviously interest in him.

– "These are buildings in which the best achievements of science and technology are held up to view," – explained Mr. Fadeev.

– "And what are plants?" – asked again Los elaborative question.

It was difficult to explain to aliens what factories were. Members of group stopped in tracks. Everybody's thoughts worked with a madden speed, processing plenty of information concerning plants into a minimum of knowledge available to the visitors. Nikolay Salkin was the first who found how to explain this complexity. He decided to ask a counter question.

– "And where do you produce your devices?"

– "At special stations," – answered Los.

– "We produce at the same stations, too, but only at our end they are called "plants"," – confirmed Mr.Salkin, and the necessity of a long and verbose explanation disappeared.

– "That's clear." – the made analogy instantly clarified everything in thoughts of aliens. – "but where are these plants located?"

– "There is a powerful plant-station near this house. There are thousands of different devices," - suggested Mr.Gromov.- "You may choose any, nobody will notice it."

– "Yes, we have understood: a premise with dozens of different devices is called the plant. We have seen two such objects. Well, we will look there."

– "You called your planet not by name, but by the number. Why is it so?" – asked Michael Fadeev. He was a mathematician, therefore he was mostly interested in figures.

– "All planets at our end are denoted not by letters, but by figures. We use other designations, than people. But do you know, I hope, what figures express?"

We were ashamed of ourselves as nobody of us knew it. Faces of many people reflected awkwardness. But it was Mr.Fadeev who ventured to recognize human ignorance.

– "I should admit, unfortunately, that we do not know it. But I do hope, you will share with us this knowledge," - he optimistically continued. – "We are your friends. And it is necessary to share knowledge with friends," - and he cunningly winked at the rests.

Aliens did not equivocate the answer. But now Edar began to reply.

– "Figures bear energy," - he informed. – "through numbers we have a distribution of energies. By means of numbers we determine, how many energy goes to this or that area. We named you a code of the planet. And it characterizes increase and decrease of energy."

– "What can you tell about a code of the person?" – Mr.Fadeev tried to approximate their knowledge to the earthly one.

– "The man has a code 9935 units. It is his/her exchange with Space," - informed Edar.

– "Do all people have it the same?"

– "All the mankind has a general code. But each man has a personal one."

That way we learnt about ourselves from other's lips. It was not clear, why others knew about us, i.e. about the person, more than we ourselves. Nevertheless, it was possible to explain it only from one point – mankind had a low level of development.

But things they told us about, could not be considered as true knowledge because we got replies from the same beings, as we ourselves. However, they knew something more, as any person, something – less. Much knowledge they mixed with their personal opinion, which was not always true for everybody. Therefore during contacts with them we more learned about their way of existence than derived new information.

– "And if to take two men, do they have different codes?" – continued to ask Alexander.

– "Yes, different."

– "What does it depend on?" - asked again he.

– "It is a numbering of your enumeration. A code of every person depends on his/her three subtle bodies close to the matter, and on a level of development. All these are added and a code turns out."

– "Is it the sum of energies?" – asked Alexander.

– "Yes. The code indicates, how much approximately energy your organism processes per year, that is so much energy in total rises in you and subsides. There is an energy circulation. And all this is calculated according to productivity of the person.

– "Great, you live entire life and even do not know that you work, as electric power station, bulbs can be connected to you," - joked Natalia.

– "And can we determine a code of the person?" – asked Mr.Fadeev.

– "No, you can't. It is difficult."

– "To increase productivity of energy, one should purify power channels, shouldn't he?" – asked again Natalia.

– "What for should you increase energy productivity? Are you lacking of it? Do you have not enough energy?" – Los was surprised.

– "I simply would like not to lag behind others,"-explained Mrs. Molodtsova.

– "Everything depends on your regular jobs. Don't you think, that if you are engaged in nothing, its receipt will increase? In that case it won't come to you at all. Its quantity will decrease to the minimum possible value. To increase its inflow, it is necessary to devote yourself to something constantly. And then you will receive so much as you need. But channels, of course, you should purify, too. For this purpose people have their ways, and we – our own."

– "Are there in your parallel worlds people?" – asked with an interest Mrs.Molodtsova.

– "People are only at your end. As for us there are beings," - answered Los.

There was a hitch with questions. The group persistently thought of what to ask our invisible beings more, what to inquire about. While they were thinking of questions, I addressed them:

– "Tell us about your social system, please."

– "What do you mean – what do we consist of?" – Los did not understand me. He decided that I had asked about the structure of their body. And not to show that he had misunderstood a question, I had to confirm his verification.

– "Yes. You have said to us that your food is energy. Therefore we would like to know. If you eat energy, hence, are there no digestive organs inside you?"

– "Yes, precisely," - confirmed Los.

– "Excuse me, but then we would like to know, what do you have inside, what organs?" – I was curious.

– "No, we won't reveal it to you for a while. We first should understand what personalities you are, whether you cause us harm or not."

Larisa showed me her hair, hinting to ask about them. Let me say, that when somebody of strangers was present she never asked questions, and sat silently only listening to what others talked. Therefore I passed her question.

– "Has hair for you any value?"

– "Yes, it is our aerials," - answered Edar.

– "But Los has no hair. How does he live without them? Has he substitutes?"

– "Hair is additional devices. He has other substitutes. They are on more subtle plane, than we ourselves, therefore your translator does not see them."

– "What do these aerials serve for? What do they catch?"

– "For us generally they are not hair, but wires," - corrected me Edar. – "Through many your devices, as we have found out, energy (tells about the current) runs. We have something similar. A power impulse runs with high speed through hair and fills our organism with energy. Hair catches energy and feed with it our body."

– "But there the current flows in wires from electric power station which produces it. But where does your hair take these impulses from? What serves as an energy source?"

– "As I have already told and now make it precise, energy is caught by hair from stars. But it is only of definite frequency. Supplying comes from stars. From your Sun. But there are stars which work in such spectrum that our hair receives from them nothing."

– "And how about the person, does hair play the same role?" – asked I.

– "We know that it is also aerials, but it has another structure, than ours. Find out yourself, what functions it holds."

– "And have Los ever had hair? Why is he bald-headed?"

– "What have you frozen to my bald head?" - Discontentedly and absolutely in a terrestrial way grumbled Los, but at the same time answered the question: - "I had hair, had. I have got into an accident, and it has burnt away. But each detail in our organism has its doublers. I catch energy in another way and feed my organism."

– "Our translator has seen your teeth. But if you feed on energy, what do you have teeth for?" - insisted I, trying to find out as much as possible about their structure, if not internal, then the external one." – "for example, the man is provided with them to bite off and chew the food."

–"These are not teeth, but special magnetic devices. They help us catching definite frequencies of energies. Therefore we see you and hear your sounds, but you don't see and hear us."

– "Besides you have also ears. Then what do you have ears for?" - insisted I, looking into their structure, almost as in "Little Red Riding Hood" fairy tale.

– "At our end these devices are called the instrument of a wide sounding. By means of it we listen to each other and we hear many other things at huge distances. You do not hear what we catch. But we can hear you far away. If we are on the opposite side of the Earth and you will call us, we will hear you with our instruments and will arrive."

– "As I have understood: the devices, which we call "teeth", help you hear at near distance, and ears – for a long distance."

– "Yes, you have properly understood our structure," - agreed Los. – "Everything concerning the Earth, is for us small distances."

– "In that case could you tell us, what the president of the United States is speaking now?" – there and then put a provocative question Michael, trying to catch them in a lie.

– "We can, but we are not familiar with this person. We should know, whom to focus on. We already know you, remember, who on what frequencies talks, and that is why can catch these frequencies. Certainly, if you inform us, what frequencies to catch, we shall tell you what the president is speaking about."

– "And will you catch sounds of his voice with your teeth?" – mistrustfully asked I.

– "These are not teeth, we have already told you. Everything concerning us, has other names and functions."

– "We symbolically name so," - reconciling said I. – "let it be magnets or devices-locators. It is important for us to know, what functions they carry out."

– "They catch low-frequency waves from a source of drawing near or leaving noise manufacture, and process the data into the information, which is clear to us."

While we were carrying on the dialogue, I noticed that Mr. Gromov activated his third eye and was immersed in own research of the subtle world. Dialogue proceeded.

– "The channeler has seen on your feet something like flippers. What are they for?"

– "These are not flippers, but special appliances, which are necessary to walk on our soil. We have a very rough soil, so you simply won't be able to go on it with your feet, you will flatten the limbs and will have the same."

– "And do you have nose for recognition of smells or also for any other purposes?" – returned again I to details of the face.

– "It is a so-called apparatus for us, too, for recognition of ethereal radiations. It is on the terrestrial plane. However on other planets it catches other radiations of objects. Our apparatus works almost as your nose, but its sensitivity is higher, than human."

– "Do you feel a wardrobe smell?" – asked with an interest Mr.Fadeev. – "We, for example, do not feel."

– "Of course," - answered Los. – "Each subject at your premise has a special smell, and everybody of us feels it."

My spouse and I all that time were standing. My feet got tired, and I began to think of where to sit. I looked at the chairs where Los together with Edar were sitting, and unexpectedly decided in my thoughts: «How about to sit down on the same chairs? If one place can combine several parallel worlds at one time why not to be joined in space. It will be rather curious». And I took the seat on the chair where Los was sitting. Actually I took the place inside him, or more precisely, within his field.

Alexander raised eyebrows in astonishment, but I gestured for him to sit down on another chair, too, understanding that he also got tired to stand. He smiled slightly, having understood a humorous situation, and sat down on the second vacant chair, taking place inside Edar.

It was clear how parallel worlds took place one inside another, but how one being did it in another one, we got a chance to experience ourselves.

As soon as I sat down, I had just felt a slight pricking from different sides: it seemed that there was an abnormal zone around, it's tension was felt."

– "Well, interesting, when Los will be speaking, shall I feel something or not?" - thought I and began to follow my feelings.

– "Can you read our thoughts?" – asked Nikolay Salkin.

– "We have already learnt much about you, so we catch something," - answered Los.

I listened to feelings, but noticed no changes in a field surrounding me.

– "So, could you read my thoughts? What am I thinking about?" – put again a provocative question Michael.

– "No, at this moment we shall tell you nothing. But we know what you are thinking about and what you are going to do," - answered Los, who didn't want to respond to the provocation.

– "But why do not you want to tell aloud my thought? Or does it confuse you?" – insisted our mathematician.

– "You want much at once, we so understand you," - Los answered laconically with mistrust to Michael in his tone.

– "No, I only want you to read my thought," - recklessly declared Mr.Fadeev. – "How will you succeed in it?"

– "It will not just be interesting, when you will know everything."

– "But I would like to know," - insisted Michael. – "Perhaps you lie, exaggerate your abilities to seem higher than we, but in reality are capable of nothing."

An accusatory tone of materialist, demanding material evidences, hurt Los, as they say, to the quick.

– "We caught your thought as soon as appeared here. You have the only one thought as you say – «to show us up in our true colors». You have come here thinking to expose us. You are of all those present the most captious. Isn't it really so?"

– "Yes, I wished to prove that you were not capable to read our thoughts and to influence a material world," - agreed Michael.

– "Influences may be different, and often such, about which you do not even suspect," - categorically declared Los.

I felt that atmosphere around me became heated. In the literal sense it was hot to me. Probably, Los was irritated by Michael's mistrust and as a response to aggression, the body temperature (or to be more exact of the field) rose.

But Michael continued trickily to provoke them to visual effect.

– "Sometimes low beings get into our world and give themselves out to be Gods, but themselves are capable of nothing. To guess my thoughts is not difficult as it is clear that every earthman would like to see you or at least to look at your influence on material subjects …"

Michael, as they say, pestered Los with his mistrust, so that he did not listen till the end, ordered:

– "Well, put a sheet of paper on your box," - he meant the TV.

Larisa quickly brought a blank sheet of paper out of the room and put it on the TV.

– "We demand attention and silence," - ordered Los.

I felt that for some time the field left me. It grew a little cooler.

Los rose, came to the TV. All those present stopped short.

The sheet trembled and began to slide slowly from a rough surface. Soon it entire slided down the TV, hang for some seconds in the air and then slowly floated to Michael. It flew over his nose, I did not know casually or purposely, then after that smoothly fell to his knees. And I felt, how heat around me increased again, so consequently Los returned on the chair.

– "Incredible," - admired Natalia.

One could see satisfaction in Michael's eyes: he succeeded to provoke invisibles to visual effect. Faces of others were shining with pleasure from the seen. And that moment I understood, that all of us were still children in their souls and how we enjoyed every even the simplest miracle.

Michael's tone became friendly benevolent at once.

– "Right now we are sure that you are present here indeed. We do not see you, but would like to feel your presence somehow. After all it can appear that we simply have imagined everything to ourselves," - and then simultaneously asked. – "Is it difficult to influence a material subject?"

– "Uneasy. As it takes immense concentration of rough range energy. Not any energy can be used to move your subjects, only this, which is the closest to your world."

– "Thank you very much for the visual effect," - I thanked on behalf of everybody. –"Our people have much pleasure from the seen."

It became absolutely hot to me. I had such an impression that I was in a boiler-house, in a steam room.

– "Tell us please, is there your ship hanging over this house right now?" – asked Nikolay Salkin.

– "Are you interested to know all at once?" – gave a short laugh Los.

– "Yes, we are."

– "Well, let us assume, is hanging."

– "You do not trust us?" – asked with an interest Mr.Salkin and assured: - "We are your friends."

– "The man is not constant in his/her opinion. Today he wants one thing, tomorrow – the opposite. And this can cause harm to us as today you are friends, and tomorrow – enemies because you will change the opinion concerning something."

– "But do you think the other way round? After all everything in our life changes, and together with it – the opinion," –answered Nikolay.

– "We know much, therefore we say what is necessary. The knowledge of truth does not allow us to change the opinion.

Heat around me became intolerable, I literally evaporated, did not bear it, rose. Next to me my spouse followed. I came to window to have a breath of fresh air. The window was opened, and a pleasant fresh air was blowing softly.

– "Our companions (he meant us) have told us that you live long," – began Mr.Gromov, who hadn't observed the invisible beings anymore and joined the conversation. – "Is there reincarnation at your end, that is how many times have you been born on the planet?"

– "The process of it is almost the same as with earthmen. We live, and die, when we merge, then a new birth follows further. Our soul flies to another world, too, and it is 10 times subtler than ours."

– "Does your soul see well the other world after death?"

– "Yes, soul's sight and also other sensations are very well developed. You, for example, now cannot see the parallel world and when your soul will leave your body, you will perceive much.

– "Do you remember your previous life or the life before the last? Or have you got, as the human, blocking?" – continued to ask Mr.Gromov.

– "It is impossible to recall, how you pass from one life to another. We only calculate that we were then and then. It is all calculated. And to recall, whom you were in the past and how you lived, it is difficult."

– "Where do your soul fly after death, do you know?" – found out I.

– "We know only that souls are collected in a definite storehouse and then they are distributed, whom-where to send further. They can transfer them to the other world."

– "Can your souls get into our world?" – addressed I again to Los.

– "No. For us it would mean coming back in development. A soul should go only forward."

– "People die with fear and unwillingness, and what do you think of death?" – showed an interest Mr.Gromov.

– "The death is a transition into the other world. It is difficult. Simply the man has not been prepared for it yet. We have had earlier fear, too, but then we have overcome it. Now it becomes a habit."

Mr.Gromov was going to ask one more question, but the aliens rose and declared:

– "We were glad to get acquainted with you. The ship is waiting for us. All the best."

We thanked them for a meeting, too. Mr.Fadeev and Mr.Salkin suggested them to meet once again. The aliens answered evasively, but did not deprive of hope, having told that if something, they would transfer the invitation to the group through us.

They left. We stayed alone. The group brightened up at once, became noisy, everybody shared impressions. Delicate Nikolay Salkin exhorted Michael that he had demanded too much from them and was insufficiently polite with the visitors.

– "Why should we bow before invisible beings? They do not understand our etiquette," - waved the matter aside Michael.

I addressed to Mr.Gromov:

– "Vladimir, what interesting have you seen?"

Mr.Gromov kindly burst out laughing:

– "Can you imagine, how it is interesting to see yourself made of another matter? It happens, that there are doubles in subtle world, too. But, as a matter of fact, it is not the most important thing. I would like to see, where they would appear from, but it was not a success: looked in one direction, and they appeared I did understand where from. And it was just interesting, how the alien moved a sheet. I thought, he would move it on a distance with his thought, but he took it in a hand and carried. But also he could not pick up it by hand at once, at the beginning it was not easy for him. And then he, probably, made an effort and it turned out. That was curious to watch. But what they speak about, unfortunately, I cannot understand."

– "Never mind, in the next life you will master clairaudience," - consoled him Michael.

Visitors shared their notes for an hour or so, and then broke up. And I decided to exchange impressions with Alexander concerning our combination with aliens.

– "How about sitting in arms of aliens?"

– "At the beginning it was ok. It became hot only towards the end."

– "I felt the same," - confirmed I. – "It became hot some time later. I thought that Los was angry or worried, and that was why the field temperature rose. But as it was found out, Edar had the same, that means it could be something else."

– "I even sweated," - admitted Alexander.

– "It is great to sit, however, in someone like a microbe," - joked I. – "Feelings were inexpressible."

– "Tell somebody, they will not believe," – said my spouse.

– "Yes," - agreed I. – "we were combined in one space point and time co-ordinates, but everyone at the same time kept his integrity and individuality. It is not clear, how does it turn out purely constructively? To explain it with a presence of dimensions, differences in frequencies, of course, is possible, but so much is hidden behind it! Human mind will not understand. – And then I came back to the present moment from philosophical categories. – "It is interesting, did our visitors feel, that hosts were – inside?"

– "They were carried away by polemic, they had no time for it," - convincingly declared Alexander.

In spite of the fact that visitors remained invisible, the meeting impressed members of our group very much, and they asked one more meeting with them. Therefore we had to promise them to arrange a meeting again.

But how could we agree with aliens if they departed, without having said, when they would return. We had to wait. An opportunity soon was presented itself.

Chapter 4

Treatment of the channeler and aliens materialization

Our friends appeared as always unexpectedly. Four days later Dmitry had to stay for the night with us. We investigated subtle world, and were so carried away that remembered about time and that it was time for the young man to go home, only at one AM. There was no transport any more, it was far to go, and at that time it was dangerous, therefore we suggested him to stay for the night. It was rather cramped in two-room flat, therefore we made a folding bed in the kitchen.

Dmitry fell asleep very quickly, we too. But approximately an hour later I woke up. I could not understand what had made me to wake up, but it seemed that I had heard some noise and so decided to check it up. I had left the light switched on in the corridor to make it visible for the visitor where he was because I understood that half asleep person could not often remember his whereabouts and what was up.

I came out to the corridor, and dropped in the kitchen. The door was open. Obviously, I got up in the right moment because I saw something unusual.

Folding bed with Dmitry, slightly rocking, was slowly rising up. It hang in the air in the middle of the kitchen, approximately, one metre over the floor.

Dmitry as it seemed to me, did not sleep. The blanket slowly slipped down from him and moved to a stool. I saw, how Dmitry's eyelids trembled, he slightly raised them, and we met our eyes. I was already going to rush to help him, but he put a finger to lips, calling me to be silent, and whispered:

– "Come in half an hour. They are curing me."

I came back to the room. My husband got up, too, and asked:

– "What's up?"

I told in a whisper what I had seen.

– "Who is curing him?" – asked Alexander that one could hardly hear.

– "I think, our aliens," - assumed I. – "Who is just interested in it".

The daughter woke up, too, and came from her room to us. We begun to wait.

In half an hour smiling Dmitry dropped and asked:

– "Have you been frightened?" – We shaken our heads. Having taken seat in an armchair, he explained. – "Los and Edar came. There were three more unknown beings together with them. Los said to me that these were repairmen of material bodies. As it turned out, when we last met they found out a gastric ulcer in me and decided to treat. So they have invited experts, and they made my ulcer cicatrized. As Philippine healers, everything was done without cutting me."

– "Are you sure, what they have treated you?" – I begun to doubt. – "Perhaps they carried out experiments, didn't they?"

– "No, they cured. I had a stomach ache for a long time. There was no time to visit a doctor," - explained the young man.

– "Are they still here?" –asked Larisa.

– "No, they, so to say, "called on the way" specially to treat me and left. But promised that were going to be here tomorrow at seven PM. They will come to check up, how are things with me."

– "Ok. We have not to forget about invitation one more time to meet with the group," - remembered I.

– "Have you felt something inside?" - The daughter asked with an interest.

– "No. As soon as you left me, I just fell asleep. I remember only as the folding bed was rising. It's an amazing feeling. Half asleep, I did not understand at once what happened. They fly by carpets-planes in fairy tales, and I – on a folding bed. It's incredible impression."

– "Before the group they only notebook sheet moved, and without witnesses – the whole folding bed with the person lifted," - noticed Larisa. – "that means, they are very strong but conceal their strength."

Dmitry explained:

– "They did not lift. One of newcomers had some device in hands, and it lifted a folding bed. I think, they do not deceive us. We should trust them."

It was necessary to prepare questions for a meeting, to make up conversation outline. But reciprocal and incidental questions arose just in the process of it and served for getting more details or broadening newcomers' answers. I was charged with all questions and had to find out constantly topics for discussion, then develop them. During all my life I never asked anybody about something neither at school, nor at institute and when teachers addressed children «Does anybody have questions?», it seemed to me that everything was clear.

Long ago in childhood I paid attention that other children constantly ask adults something, as for me I held my tongue, kept quiet and that was all. Now it is clear –I have never asked questions before, to ask continuously everybody later on, since 1990, during next ten years: aliens and Hierarchical Systems, God and Devil.

At that time our group was conducting contacts with Higher Teachers, Hierarchical Systems "the Union". I prepared questions for them, and now in absolutely another foreshortening I had to make up questions for aliens so I needed to feel that questions to the later had completely different subjects, and sense. To some beings we could talk about one topic, to others – about others. But the most important thing – we should learn more new to correlate, compare with a human life, to learn something from them, and to transfer something to them. The sense of all these conversations, sense of our meetings consisted in learning to communicate with different Levels of development, different forms of existence, and learning to understand everybody.

Our talks were not idle conversations of weary representatives of two different worlds. Meetings had educational character. But I understood it, of course, much later. We should develop in ourselves feeling of other beings, investigate the worlds invisible to us and compare them to ours. But the most important thing, was to learn to find common concepts between absolutely different: between quality of the matter and structure of the worlds, between a way of life and a level of other beings perception. And then transform this common into something frequently used for two worlds.

No doubt, the meeting with aliens was not casual: it was arranged by our Higher Teachers.

They simply gave us a chance to meet with representatives of two different worlds and to find out things in common, common topics for conversation. The Higher kept an eye on us from the Above and analyzed our ability to communicate with forms of life from another plane of existence, to talk actually to such illusory (especially for fierce materialists) world, as subtle one.

There was an experiment on their side, too: neither we, nor Los and Edar knew that we had been brought together in one space point specially and each step of both parties was controlled. But I found it, of course, much later.

This questions and answers game should connect different worlds in concepts. It was studies for three of us. And it helped the daughter to form fundamental base of semantic categories for reception and decoding of the difficult information later.

But while the Higher kept an eye on us from the Above, I was preparing questions. By appointed hour they had been made up.

Dmitry came at seven PM and informed:

– "The ship arrived, it is hanging over the house. Soon guests will welcome." – and literally in two minutes channeler declared: - "They have come. Los has sat in an armchair, Edar is standing near him, has put his elbows on a high back of the armchair and, of course, is staring at Larisa. After all he has arrived specially because of me, and looks at her. Outrageous!" - Grumbled the young man.

– "He looks through her," - joked I.

Dmitry got into the mood for contact and informed:

– "They are sending greetings to everybody. They have offered me to sit on a sofa for examination and taking measurements. After that they will talk to you."

We stood still and waited. Examination was quick. Approximately three minutes later Dmitry pleased us:

– "I am fine, there is no ulcer. But they have told – not to eat rough food for a week. That's all. Now they ask, what would you like to know?"

– "We are interested, what's their impression after a meeting with the group?" – addressed the channeler I.

– "Impression is so-so. There were people who did not trust us," - replied Los. One could hear discontent in his tone.

I tried to defend:

– "You see, it's for the first time when they meet such beings, as you. There are too many swindlers and liars in our world, who have deceived them, therefore it is difficult to believe what they do not see. But it's not the point. After all our spiritual evolution is younger than yours, therefore, as all children, the person loves some miracles. Here you moved a sheet of paper from one end to another, and it was such a joy for everybody, you gave them pleasure."

My explanation made on them a pleasant impression.

– "Really? Well, if so we forgive those who did not trust us," - his intonation was softened.

Alexander, wishing to strengthen a positive effect, added:

– "Our people have not seen such for all their life and never will see. They will remember it till the end of life and will tell about it to their grandchildren, and great-grandchildren."

– "Who are these grandchildren and great-grandchildren?" - politely inquired Los. – "Are they from any society?"

– "They are children two generations forward. Children of the future," - explained Alexander.

The alien understood.

– "You have made a great impression on our members of the group. They dream to meet you once again," - I put in.

And our guests could not refuse after so many laudatory words in their address.

– "Well. We will come," - agreed Los.

– "To understand better each other, it is necessary to meet more often," - supported us the daughter.

Edar brightened at once. Just before it he had thoughtfully stood in the same pose, having put his elbows on the armchair back, and had only listened.

– "You are absolutely right. When you regard people in a detached spirit, from heights of the ship, they seem such limited and rigid. (Obviously, he wanted to say "hard". They sometimes made mistakes in our terminology). But since we began to talk to you, I have changed my opinion. People became interesting to me."

– "We have heard, that there are many different aliens on the Earth, but why they do not establish contact with people?" – addressed him Larisa.

Eyes of Edar were burning with mysterious unearthly light. He looked at the earthly woman thoughtfully and sadly.

– "Many aliens are much more higher in development than the human and that is why people are not interesting for them. What could they, actually, talk about? They do not even know about a subtle structure, not speaking about subtle worlds. They do not know also that there are beings almost on each planet. The man does not know much and does not wish to know. He/she is cowardly and aggressive. All this does not make them well disposed towards contacts with people."

– "But, I do hope, after the meeting with us you will change the opinion about all mankind." - smiled Larisa.

– "Yes," - agreed Edar. – "We see that people are all very different, and there are a lot of benevolent among them."

While Larisa was talking to Edar, Alexander took the bioframe in hands and began to investigate fields of our visitors.

Los at once became interested in his work.

– "I see, you make some researches. What do you check?"

– "I measure your subtle bodies and try to determine, how you are shown up in the physical world. What changes with your arrival in our room," - explained my husband.

– "Yes, it is interesting. Could you then report us about the researches," - asked Los.

– "Yes, if it is interesting to you," - agreed Alexander and proceeded the work.

– "Do you know the reason why a world can bother beings living in it?" – I asked. – "or can they like one world eternally?"

– "Why do you ask it?" – inquired in turn Los.

– "Some people say that the terrestrial world bothers separate persons, because during channelings they contact the forces of darkness and those allegedly inspired them with disgust to all around," - explained I.

– "It is the next delusion of the man," - assured Los and continued: - "Yes, sometimes it happens that beings are bothered with that world in which they live. It may be, first, if it has got all the necessary types of energy and it has nothing more to do in it. The being has to go to another, higher world and then development will continue further. The lack of interest indicates that a being has spiritually grown from the given world. And secondly, the world becomes uninteresting to it, when its life program comes to the end."

– "However can dark essences influence it, instil into it anything negative?" – reminded I.

– "They influence only low Levels of development. They have not enough power for high ones. Besides, according to general space laws nobody has the rights to interfere with another's life. Don't you know, that there are very strict laws in Space? Those, who do not know and follow them, are not allowed to fly."

– "What equipment do you use on the planet?" – To be more clear, what I am asking about, for comparison I have given an example: - "On the Earth, let us assume, there are cars, planes."

– "At our end, basically, there are ships, small space ships," - Los said tenderly, and I understood that he loved their spaceship very much. – "but there are also other ships, which fly with high speed."

– "I would like to get more details, can you or any other essence have an individual transport, a small car belonging only to you?"

– "Everybody of us has its own personal apparatus. When it is required to move at big distances, we use it."

– "What kind of fuel does it use?"

– "This energy is unknown to the person. For your rough world it is inapplicable. Usually we use not the only one kind of fuel, but several. It is very convenient. One fuel runs out, we use another. Besides, one kind of fuel is used for small distances, another – for big."

– "Is atomic energy used on your planet?"

– "It is very dangerous. It is applied only in researches. There are enough other types of energy, which are safe."

– "Could you please be more precise and tell particularly, what energy, besides star, do you use?"

– "The whole world around is different types of energy. Every being uses that one, which is available for its reason."

– "Last night you lifted Dmitry in the air, hence, are you able to influence our matter?" – asked point-blank I.

– "Yes."

– "Hence, you are familiar with its properties, aren't you?"

– "We are, as it is lower level of the matter."

– "But then, obviously, you can be materialized, can't you?" – I tried to worm out aliens possibilities hidden from us.

– "We can," – had to confess Los. – "But we have to hide from people. If you only showed up among them or even in your group, they would give us no peace. They will carry out some experiences. The human does not perceive other forms of body. Although we are similar to you, but in many respects differ from you. One day, when we arrived in a country on the opposite side of the planet I decided to get acquainted with the so-called scientist. He, at first sight, was suitable for us if to judge believes," - told Los. – "When he saw me, fell down in a dead faint, that is in your language lost consciousness. We had to bring him round. But we haven't shown up for him any more. He lost our respect. Is he really a scientist?! No, such beings at our end are not given any ranks."

Los, obviously, remembered this history, purposefully to prevent our request to materialize for us, because I just further was going to offer their appearance to us. But that story did not frighten us. For a long time we were going to ask them to show up in our world, and that moment was the most suitable for this purpose.

– "You appeared unexpectedly, therefore he was frightened. But we are already enough prepared for a meeting with you. Is it possible for you to be materialized? We would like to have complete idea about you."

– "Sure," - unexpectedly quickly agreed Los. – "Only preliminary you should promise us not to tell anybody from your group about it, otherwise they will pester us with their requests.

– "Well, we will tell nobody," - promised I.

– "And the others will not tell?" – He just for the sake of good order asked the present.

– "No doubt, we will keep silence too," - on behalf of the daughter and Dmitry assured Alexander.

– "We trust you. Prepare for our appearance. We want to warn – there can be noise and the temperature indoors will change. Move further away, please," - Los pointed out to a front wall. There was a thermometer on it, and I just in case noticed, what temperature it indicated. All four of us we leant against a wall. – "Are you ready?" – asked Los.

– "Yes," - I answered for everybody.

– "Now we will examine conditions round us," - warned Los. – "We do not want to have witnesses in our world. We had to wait for approximately three minutes and then the command sounded:

– "Be attentive. Concentrate yourself to see other beings. We are different, but we are your friends." – he became silent. Intense silence reigned. It lasted more than a minute. But what did everyone of us endure during that time? Indeed, there are minutes which are worth of the whole life.

Our slowed-down reactions, unfortunately, were not capable to catch all that occurred promptly. Organs of vision and hearing fixed only the final stage of the phenomenon.

A slight pop was heard, we felt a warm wave, it resembled a small explosion. Smell in the room also changed, more precisely, appeared together with scarcely perceptible flash, but it was difficult to tell what it reminded. And after that we saw, how Los and Edar began to show up. It was like on a film, the only difference was that their bodies were shown not plainly, but dimensionally. At first there were their silhouettes, as if made of haze, without details. During few seconds they began to show up more and more well-defined. We simply were dumbfounded with admiration.

I do not know, why the scientist fell when saw Los. Most likely there worked simply the effect of unexpectedness, but we were delighted with their materialization. Their forms soon were shown completely.

There were two smiling beings in front of us. Being materialized, they appeared to be for some reason higher than in the subtle world. Edar was approximately two metres high, and Los - somewhere metre seventy. Their form precisely coincided with that description made by Dmitry, therefore we were completely ready to the seen.

Eyes of aliens were sparkling with mysterious light: Los – derisively-indulgently, Edar - burning with passion, as if internal fire burnt him down, and that sight fully corresponded to his romantic, keen-witted nature. There was grief deeply hidden in big Edar's eyes, unlike small round eyes of Los where determination and practical nature manifested itself.

The skin of open areas of their body was streaked with a greyish-metal tint. Feet-flippers, palms with fingers of one length, muscles of the body fitted by a fine fabric of overalls – all these were perceived normally. And at the same time (likely, with the sixth sense) we felt heterogeneity of the matter and some internal power. It seemed, we felt with entire body that there was an alien organism near us, something strange in structure and quality of the matter. Edar looked stately handsome, despite foreignness of our matters. Los was more common, but also one could feel power and a high order of intelligence inside.

«No, - flashed in my mind, - such internal power the man has not».

For some seconds we silently contemplated each other. Obviously, we also looked a bit another way, than from the subtle world. We were standing and looking at each other: they at us – with a half-smile, we at them, as they say, with widely open eyes.

Our guests broke the silence first. They spoke using not sounds, but some waves because everyone of us heard words of the speaker inside him/herself. It could be named telepathy, but if to compare with human it had a special clearness of concepts arising in brain. There were not words, but concepts. Probably, it was a standard space way of communication between different by the form beings. Thus, we could manage already without a translator in the person of Dmitry.

– "How's your health?" – Los asked with an interest.

I, at last, came to my senses and tried to smile very friendly to show that they were materialized not in vain.

– "Fine," - I answered and paid a compliment to both: - "You look well. Even if to judge by human standards, you have a perfect appearance."

– "So I do say that we look not badly. It is not clear, why people are frightened," – joyfully said Edar. He was sincerely happy that his appearance did not frighten us. Eyes of the alien lighted up, I would say, with childlike light of happiness.

– "But how is it possible for you?" – I was curious.

– "We have codes," - answered Edar, - "we know the code of your matter and the formula of transition from one dimension to another."

– "Do you feel any unpleasant sensations during transition from one world to another?" – I was interested.

– "Of course, we overcome the same altitude sickness, as your cosmonauts at the moment of a landing," - informed Los.

– "Ohhhooo," - drawled I, - "then it turns out, that we have made you feel unpleasant sensations, haven't we?"

– "Never mind. We got used to feel the most different sensations, so altitude sickness for us is usual during flight," - assured Edar. – "And I would like to show people very much, that they are not right, when are afraid of us. By the way, what results do you have?" – He addressed to Alexander.

– "I have measured indicators of your subtle bodies. All of them appeared to be higher than the most possible known by the human. Your spiritual body energy power is three times higher, than common people have. Moreover, I have found out existence of three more subtle bodies. Why do you have three more subtle bodies in comparison with people?"

– "Don't you really know it?" – was surprised Los.

– "Unfortunately, no," - answered confusedly Alexander.

– "You must know that the higher the being is by the Level of development, the more subtle bodies it has," - explained Los.

– "Thank you very much, now we know it."

– "Representatives of your group must also know that," - strictly said Los. – "As some your people think that we are low beings. Only why do these "low" fly saucers from other galaxies, and "higher" are not capable to rise even from the planet? Who knows nothing, that considers himself to be very high. Certainly, we are not so-called angels who are adored by people, but we are also able much. If you are not afraid of us, then we will do so that you will see and hear us," - assured he.

– "How will you manage it?" – asked with an interest Larisa.

– "We shall only for a while make your subtle constructions catch our frequency of radiations. So it will be easier for us to communicate with you," - declared Los.

Edar appealed to Larisa as always to play the electro piano.

– "We would like to listen to music in a material body," - he explained their desire. – "We have to compare."

She could not refuse, and our guests and we came to her room. Larisa led the way, visitors – behind her, and then three of us followed them. I paid attention that in comparison with us it was difficult for guests to go and their feet-flippers made funny flapping sound, reminding me crow's feet. I was interested in the way of their moving in different environments, therefore, when we came to the room, I asked:

– "What do you feel while moving in a material body?" Is it easier for you to move or vice versa?"

– "More difficult," - admitted Los. – "I have such an impression that I gained too much weight. It is hard to raise hands, feet. We do not like your environment. When we are in our dimension we do not feel weight of the body and we move easily, freely.

I thought that, obviously, they feel, as our divers at the bottom of the sea, after all aliens got into denser environment, than their own. An idea stroke me that they for our sake, wishing to show themselves, overcame such hardships: stood immense exertions and, probably, risky as not always everything could turn out. And that moment they had to endure for the sake of our pleasure so much unpleasant sensations. Therefore I decided not to offer them any more similar experiments, and then asked with an interest:

– "Could you go on a water surface?"

– "In material body - no, but in ours – as much as you wish," - answered Los. – "Transformed in our matter, we get all its properties."

Larisa took her seat at a small piano, conversation stopped for a while. First chords made us to lapse into silence. Visitors began to listen. Now it was possible with our own eyes to look at faces of the guests, and see how music impressed them.

Their mimicry did not change. The only changes were in expression of the eyes, because their souls sounded and shone in time with the melody. It seemed, each note found the echo in the depth of their hearts.

We had listened to some melodies. Then Larisa unexpectedly offered Edar.

– "How do you like my instrument? I present it to you. You may take it on the ship."

– "Oooohh, it is a big gift. You are a kind soul. But I cannot take this instrument from you."

– "But why?" – Larisa was surprised.

– "First of all, because it is your favourite instrument. And I know what is it to lose your favourite instrument. I cannot give you grief. And secondly, we are not allowed to bring from other planets any things. But not to afflict you, allow me to play for you a melody of our planet."

– "Sure, it is very interesting to listen to the alien music," - Larisa gave up her place at the electro piano to him.

Edar played at once, somehow he immediately mastered the instrument. A wonderful melody, tender and mysterious, exciting and bearing something far and not clear for us, enigmatic and illusive, poured. The melody enchanted, but Edar hadn't managed to finish it to the end: something loudly clicked in the piano, and it stopped. It appeared, that it burnt out, as did not sustain the tension coming from the musician. He was disappointed.

– "I have broken your instrument! It's a pity! You have not listened to my music up to the end."

– "Don't take it to heart, we shall repair "Elektrino"," - Larisa tried to console. But Edar promised:

– "By the morning I will repair it myself, do not worry. I will finish my song later. And now it is time for us to leave. We will go to another your premise and transform to a former state. Come in five minutes. Returning is more difficult."

They said goodbye and left.

Silently we were listening to that hidden from us behind walls. What was happening there? How was dematerialization done: whether the material body crumbled to components, whether one was transformed into another, or there was something else more incredible for our consciousness? We heard a small explosion, but it was more powerful, than the first, even glasses began to rattle in a set of furniture.

– "Neighbours will be indignant – we make much noise," - whispered Alexander.

– "We shall tell – a book shelf has broken off the wall," - also in a whisper answered I.

In a definite time purely with curiosity after them we returned to a drawing-room. It was empty. At first sight nothing told that there had been a mysterious case there.

I looked at the thermometer on a wall. The temperature on it was two degrees below. Air in the room was as in a thunder-storm after the lightning. Obviously, the quantity of ozone increased. It was everything what we could fix, as they say, with the naked eye.

And despite aliens had left, next day the electro piano worked. Obviously, some contact or a wire had burnt out, and Edar repaired it, having proved that they had a good understanding of any our equipment, and not just TVs. But their bent for any, even insignificant technical inventions, was obvious. They could not pass indifferently not only by a simple alarm clock, but even by a tiny watch. So, during the appointed meeting with the group Dmitry noticed that while Edar was answering questions, Los was zealously probing Alexander's watch, having been left on the table.

The next meeting took place in due time. The present were the same, and together with us there were ten persons. Not to be combined in dimensions, that time I asked neighbours to give us two stools so everyone sat on a separate place.

The group came an hour earlier, everybody liked to talk to representatives of other planet. While they were not, people shared impressions about last meeting. Natalia as usually joked:

– "I feel with the astral body that Edar is handsome. But I am old for him, and Los by the age is just for me. Do they need terrestrial wives? It would be good to ask."

– "It is necessary to think more globally," - in tone to her joked Mr.Gromov, - "If they are same-sex, let's do them an offer – to take away all old women to their planet. There are more women here than men. We shall level the population."

– "Old women, why so?" - Natalia did not understand.

– "They are thousand years old, and our old women are only seventy. They are just girls for them."

– "No, whatever you may say," - sighed Natalia, - "with Los I even to the world's end shall fly. He is a positive man it is felt at once.

I have dreamt about such for all my previous twenty lives. And here I have been palmed off a drunkard. I haven't seen our world because of him. But with Los I would run around the galaxy, would help him, teach to eat our millet pudding."

– "Why millet ?" – Mr.Salkin was surprised.

– "I like it and want him also to take a liking to it. With butter you know, how tasty it is."

In such approximately playful tone they were chattering and further when Dmitry declared:

– "They have come. Take places. Sending you their greeting."

A confidential meeting begun.

Nikolay Salkin as the most delicate of all those present, addressed them with gratitude words:

– "Allow me to thank you on behalf of our group for paying attention to us. We understand, that each minute is worth much for you and that you have a lot of work to do, so the more valuable this meeting for us is. Many thanks."

– "We are glad that you appreciate our communication. Not all people are capable of it. And you have precisely expressed the situation," - answered Los. – "We are ready to answer your questions. What are you interested in?"

– "Last time we advised to look for the device necessary to you at our station. Have you found something suitable?" – asked the first question Mr.Salkin.

– "No. But we have found what we need, in the commonwealth of people named Japan. They have advanced machinery, it surpasses yours. We have visited your station and have seen a total mess. Such disorder we haven't seen yet. Everything is scattered or piled not clearly how. Who are these heads if they allow such lack of system and mess at the station?"

– "We have reorganization now," - I began to defend those heads, whose hide nor hair I had never seen. – "it is difficult for them to keep an eye on all, because everything changes very quickly. Many people master their job for the first time, they have not enough experience yet. Stations pass to the new form of work. And in such conditions it is hard to put things in order at once." – (I remind that our meeting with aliens took place at the end of 1992).

– "We have reorganization moments too, but the order is maintained. Everything depends on your heads. At our end such ones would never admitted close to stations." - disorder on another planet for some reason continued to worry Los.

Wishing to divert him from unpleasant impression, I asked:

– "And in Japan – is that a device you need or is it analogue?"

– "Analogue. All devices should be arranged to our environment and purposes of using. You apply them for one purposes, and we – for others. But we have found premises in Japan, in which there is an order and there are many similar devices."

– "Have you *whistled* (translator's notes: in Russian colloquial speech "to whistle" means "to steal")*one?" – Mr.Fadeev asked directly laying stress on a local dialect.

– "What does it mean "whistled"?" – did not understand Los. – "We are not birds and do not whistle."

– "I say – have you taken for yourself one among a set?" - softly and cunningly-insinuatingly our materialist found out.

– "We take nothing, we draw schemes, and fix a device principle," - answered Los.

And here Dmitry just saw that Los came nearer to Alexander's watches lying on the table and began to investigate.

– "I so understand that you are technical spies," – triumphantly declared Mr.Fadeev, rejoicing that he understood their essence. –"All novelties you take for yourselves."

– "Tell me please…No lie! Is "spies" a dirty word?" – asked Edar, feeling in the word some nasty trick.

Not wishing to offend aliens, Mr.Fadeev immediately began to disguise imminent conflict.

– "No, don't say so! This is a very good word. The best intelligence men on the Earth, who pick up useful information for people are called so."

– "Yes, yes," – agreed with him Mr.Gromov. – "a spy is an intelligence man of first class."

But, strangely enough, in two unknown concepts Edar caught negative sense in the term "spy" and positive - in the word "intelligence man" and chose for himself the latest.

– "We are intelligence men because we work by the order of our Supreme leaders, but for the benefit of our beings," - he answered, but, having remembered the previous meeting, asked at once: - "Perhaps you know any other interesting devices, don't you?"

Despite the materialistic basis constantly demanding real evidences, Michael was prone to noble impulses and good deeds. That time he brought with himself a dictaphone for recording talks but when the alien asked about devices, he, without a moment's hesitation, offered:

– "I can present you a dictaphone after our meeting," - he showed a black box lying on his knees. – " I will take a cassette for myself, and the rest - welcome to it."

– "Ok, we will take an etheric cover of your thing if you do not really pity. Please think it over," - warned Los.

– "Why should I pity? I will buy new," - Michael had wanted to say: «No matter, it is outdated», but refrained in time, having understood that a gift in that case would not turn out. – "but what does it mean – «to take an etheric cover»?" – he was curious.

– "This means that we shall take a subtle structure on which your rough matter reposes, and your box will quickly crumble."

– "For your sake I do not pity," - smiled Michael.

– "Is there money in your society?" – Practical and especially materialistic, asked Mr.Gromov.

– "Money? What does it mean?"

– "Money is valuable pieces of paper, which make it possible to get different things." – Mr.Gromov took out of a trouser pocket ten roubles and showed to the visitors.

Their reaction appeared unexpected. Edar suddenly rocked with uncontrollable laughter, and his emotions were so strong that members of the group felt, as a light wind blew in the room. He laughed, likely, the whole minute. Dmitry commented:

– "He is shaking with laughter, as a leaf on the wind. He thrown back his head and guffaws, as a horse."

– "What is the second doing?" – Natalia asked with an interest.

– "He is already rummaging in Michael's box. He is likely tearing etheric cover out of it. He does not pay attention to Edar. He is serious."

– "And did he find so ridiculous in money?" - Shrugged shoulders puzzled Mr.Gromov. – "Perhaps, I have shown to him not much."

However Edar, at last, ceased laughing and commented:

– "Do you consider this empty piece of paper valuable? In three earthly days it will decay. There are organic substances in it, and it cannot be of interest for any alien beings, trust my thousand-year experience."

–"It is a conditional value," - began to explain Mr.Gromov, seeing that point of view of different beings concerning one issue could be opposite. What seems valuable to some beings, is subject to derision of the others."

– "But how do you get then things necessary for life in your world?" – My spouse came to the rescue Mr.Gromov.

– "Everything in our world is for free, there are no pieces of paper. Everyone takes what and how much he needs. But nobody takes more than necessary and unnecessary too. We have noticed that people in their dwellings have a lot of unnecessary things. Do you specially work for them?" – Edar was surprised.

– "And what do you consider unnecessary?" –timidly inquired Natalia, and anxiety appeared for some reason in her eyes.

– "There are so many soft things at your buildings, we heard, people call them "clothes". Those things which you put on feet, one person may have ten pieces. And we would have only one."

– "But your ones are, likely, durable, and ours are full of holes or with worn out toe caps," - Natalia began to defend herself, having understood that Edar said about shoes.

– "How have you reached such a welfare, that everyone gets what he needs?" – asked I. – "Here such relations are called communistic. People were going to construct a similar society, but they had no success."

– "For this purpose a high consciousness of every being is required. It is necessary to understand and see many consequences of your own actions. More often people think only about themselves, and at our end everyone thinks about everybody. We have made such life by ourselves. Economy and building are controlled constantly. If something wrong, we together put them to rights. If you try, you can achieve the same. To do life better for everyone, one should do good for all. But people somehow go another way. One tries to do good for him/herself and as a result everybody suffers and becomes despondent."

I was pleased very much with Edar's simple discourse. His consciousness resembled consciousness of our individual – the builder of communism. Hence, those relations for which we worked, were not illusion. We went correctly, but somewhere halfway turned aside.

– "So do you think, that it is far for people to such society?" – asked I.

– "I think that these are relations of the future for you. The mankind has not matured spiritually for such relations yet," - firmly declared Edar.

– "Do you consider, that the human consciousness should grow for a long time?" – found out Alexander. – "Every man considers that he/she is super intelligent."

– "People have young souls. Why should they have a high consciousness," - objected Edar. – "For one life at once, even long life, it is impossible to learn all."

At that time our translator unexpectedly exclaimed with astonishment:

– "Oho! A girl has appeared and precisely the same, as we. Amazingly. She does not resemble anybody of them."

Los entered the conversation. Having left his favourite "device", he decided to explain the presence of a new member of their crew.

– "She is our colleague. She conducts research of people. Last time you measured us with a device, we decided to take measurements too. Do not worry, they are harmless. However each party studies what is interesting to it. We will derive mutual benefit from our meetings. I do hope, you do not mind, do you?"

I casted a glance at the present. They nodded that they were not against of it. Mr.Gromov only asked Alexander:

– "What measurements did you make?"

– "We checked their subtle bodies. And by the way, their spiritual indicators, and also mental ones appeared much more higher, than human."

– "Now it's clear. Let them, of course, measure," - waved his hand Mr.Gromov. – "Nothing to lose. It is an obvious fact that aliens are interested in our indicators, and we – in theirs."

– "Certainly, let them measure. You may begin with me," - cheerfully offered Natalia. – "Only first of all introduce your girl, please."

– "This is Anfrida, the youngest among us. She carries out a certain work on the ship."

– "Dmitry, describe us the girl, please," – asked I.

– "She – is pretty, has a long blonde plait, from the waist down. A dress is red, below the knees, fitting. There is a collar above. She holds some violet box with buttons in her hands."

Directing this box at every person, the girl clicked buttons. Her measurements looked simple.

– "What indicators do you read?" – asked I.

– "Psycho-physical," - Los shortly answered, but it explained to us little.

– "The direction is known, but it is not clear what it will give to them," – said Mr.Salkin.

– "Could we get acquainted with the girl closer?" – Michael cheerfully offered. Presence of the alien encouraged him and set his heart on lyrics. He was unmarried, handsome and had many girl-friends.

– "What are you interested in?" – strictly asked Los.

– "How old is she?" – Michael showed his interest.

– "In accordance with our measures – three hundred eighty."

– "Wow! So old!" – the materialist was surprised. – "but why does she look so young? There is a contradiction."

– "Because our time does not coincide with yours," - laconically answered Los, and in his tone dissatisfied «Cannot you really guess such a trifle» appeared. He added aloud: - "Our time is incommensurate with yours."

– "Well, let's say, she is so many years old, as she looks," - Michael agreed and addressed the translator: - "Dmitry, how old is she in accordance with earthly measures? We shall determine commensurability strictly by sight.

– "Eighteen," - Dmitry determined.

– "Let's consider so. And where is she from?"

– "Please, do not ask about it. It is our secret," - discontentedly said Los.

– "But do you have the same girls else?" – Could not stop the materialist.

– "No, she is the only one. But we ask not to find out anything regarding this issue," - categorically repeated Los. – "Are you interested in something else?"

We had to change urgently the topic.

– "Do you wear another clothes on the planet or do you go in similar overalls?" – asked I.

– "Of course, we have some clothes, but no-frills. On our planet there can be both warm, and cold. We also as people, have to protect the body. But such dampness and dirt like on the Earth, we havn't."

Los meant frequent rains on the Earth. There was late autumn, rains followed rains, it was wet and dirty outside.

– "Dirt here is because of dust existence and small soil particles. So, don't you really have dust?" – I again asked.

– "We have not enough water, not enough liquid. What is the dust?" – Los asked with an interest, causing smiles of most those present.

– "These are small particles got split off our planet. It is called "the soil", on which we walk outside. It consists of small particles which in heat turn into dust, and when it is raining – into dirt," - explained I.

– "We have another soil, there is no dust on it. Soil is dense and rough."

– "Do your stations release poisons and smoke into the atmosphere or are they filtered, I mean are specially cleaned with any facilities?"

Having said the word "filtration", I caught myself thinking that it would be new and incomprehensible for them, therefore it was necessary to give an additional explanation, so I did. The peculiarity of their perception was that if we simply said an unknown term, they did not understand it and asked further explanations. But if there was some explanations after the term or any semantic addition, they understood everything well. Therefore that time, despite there was more difficult word being said, than the word "dust", it was clear for them. And Los answered:

– "We have special services, which strictly control wastes. Nobody spoils the air. Each station has a powerful system of filtration. The nature is not polluted, although it is much poorer than yours. Everything what we build, is better adapted for life. But at the same time there is a strict discipline and a high responsibility."

– "You have said that you are attacked sometimes by beings from other planet. It means, that you should have your own army and special beings, who defend you, is it so?" – addressed to Los Alexander. – "On Earth, for example, such beings are called soldiers. They wear special clothes and, by the way, have special fighting equipment. Have you been interested in it?"

– "We know your soldiers. Their equipment is very primitive. It is a machinery of savages. It kills and destroys. We do not use such. Our equipment, as we have already told, does not kill, but only neutralize. In this regard we outran far away in comparison with Earth dwellers. We do not have a special army. We simply have experts, who are in charge of a security device, they build some constructions protecting us."

– "But how do you do without soldiers?" –Was surprised Alexander. – "That is why they butt in because they know there is nobody to defend your beings."

– "When it is necessary, each of us becomes a soldier," -objected Los.

– "However, can you adopt something useful from our military technology for yourselves?" – asked I.

– "Do you know, how much we have surpassed you technically!" – exclaimed Edar with some reproach so that I even felt awkward for my ignorance. – "The difference between ours and yours is the same, as between a spear of a savage and your weapon."

– "But how then can we explain your interest in munitions factories?" – I asked with an interest.

– "We are interested in factories not because of weapon, but of separate details," - corrected Edar. – "But, of course, we keep an eye on what level of development the person reached in military science."

At that moment Natalia sneezed and apologized.

– "Sorry, a microbe has climbed in the nose."

– "Who is microbe?" – Los tried to worm out at once.

–"It is a small being causing illnesses in the man," - tried to explain Natalia.

– "Are you ill from any beings? Why?" – The alien did not understand.

– "And how about you, aren't you ill?" – In my turn asked them I.

– "We are not ill from beings, but we have every possible damages of material and subtle bodies. We have accidents."

– "But if you arrive on our or other planet, you can quite pick up germs and be taken ill. These microbes will get into your organism and start to destroy it," - Natalia began to explain.

– "Your microbes are made of the matter, which is much lower by frequency and potential, than ours, therefore they cannot penetrate a higher one. But just in case we use as preventive measures codes with a higher potential, than our matter. By means of these codes sterilization of our organism is carried out. You know that it is possible to burn the low with a greater potential."

– "Great," – admired Natalia. If Michael lighted up while mentioning girls, Natalia – while mentioning new ways of treatment. She had already tried on herself many terrestrial methods, but nothing helped. However she did not lose hope that would find her own method of organism recovery, therefore asked at once: - "Could you please borrow us a code for germs eradication?"

– "Our codes cannot affect human body. You have absolutely another matter. But the protection code is intended for a definite energy structure, for certain parameters."

– "Please, give, I shall try. Maybe it will suit," - insisted Natalia. – "But not to do harm to the rest, I'll tell nobody about. I'll try only on myself, I promise."

– "Ok. We'll try to find a code suitable for your structure and then we shall convey. But now it is time to leave. We say thank you for your consent to allow us taking measures from you," - solemnly said Los.

– "A small matter! If you need to take some more else measures, I am always ready," - Natalia responded at once, trying to get on the right side of our invisible beings and to receive a code.

Soon aliens left. The group stared noise, sharing impressions.

– "I felt that someone approached me and stirred hair on my head," – said emotionally Mr.Salkin. The touch of aliens excited feelings and flurried thoughts. – "Perhaps it is Anfrida who makes an experiment," – assumed he.

– "She took three your hairs for herself as a keepsake," - joked Michael.

But Dmitry confirmed sensations of Mr.Salkin:

– "Anfrida really approached him and put the device on his head. And then she also approached Vladimir. Maybe, she compared something."

– "If we meet them five times or so, our sensitivity will develop so much, that we shall feel them about five metres away from us and shall begin to predict earthquakes," - joked Mr.Salkin, musefully smiling. – "but where is our girl from if they are same-sex? It is a riddle. And they do not want to explain."

– "Probably, a baby died on the Earth and when his/her soul flew out, they captured it to themselves. Other subtle bodies remained, so she appears in them," – assumed I. – "Anfrida's soul can be human if the form is similar to us."

– "Yes, a mysterious girl,"- Michael said thoughtfully. – "If I could talk to her face to face. Does she see me? Or I am only a foggy cloud for her?"

– "They told that see us dually: both material body and subtle one. Although there is selectivity in organs of perception, that is they cannot see what disturbs or distracts from work," - began to explain I. – "however human vision is designed similarly, although it is more primitive. We selectively see what is one meter or kilometer away from us, it depends on what we shall concentrate. We can blow our own trumpet ..." – laughed I, trying to find suitable comparison: before whom can the man boast? But Natalia playfully suggested:

– "... before cats and dogs."

– "Yes, it is possible so," – agreed I, – "they do not see what is in kilometer from them. And the main reason of it is that they do not need it. They live in a narrow world. And besides, to see far, one should expand understanding of the world, otherwise when you will look into the distance, you will perceive wood as a foggy cloud and houses far away you will take for a small group of stones."

Photo 1. Multiprobe is shielded by a protective field which was shown up in a specific luminance of an oval form. The ship hang over a glade and for human eyes remained invisible. It was found out only when photos were made on a high sensitivity photography film.

One can see Y.A.Shishkin's and A.I.Strelnikov's silhouettes, carrying out biolocation district research on the place of UFO ship landing.

In this place a spiral frame rotated, as a propeller from powerful radiations emanating from the ship. Alexander's biofield increased seven times after research of the given place. He felt a big energy surge and vivacity and had a good mood during the next week.

Photo 2. Enthusiasts-researchers: Y.A.Shishkin and M.Gerasimov. They are in the place of UFO machine landing. Photography film fixed a powerful energy radiation invisible for the naked eye of the man, emanating from UFO (on the top central part of the frame).

A clairvoyant found out a descent machine for one being.

Pictures were taken at daytime, in cloudy weather when there was no sun at all.

Photo 3. Alexander Strelnikov carries out biolocation measurement in the place of UFO landing.

The camera has fixed two energetic essences accompanying him during the work. Aliens, being invisible, are observing how he takes measurements.

Essences are located above his head and move in the air after the man. In that case they are without any ship. They possess the ability to move in the air environment freely, but slowly. Flying machines are used by them for high-speed movements at long distances.

Photo 4. M.Gerasimov.
Researching the place of UFO landing.

Multiprobe flew away or rose into inaccessible for the camera zone. But a mini ship (on the left) and two aliens (on the right) from this mini ship stayed above the head of the researcher. Hanging over a head, they observe the man. It is a comic situation when the person tries to find them, but they are above.

Photo 5. Larisa Seklitova is on the left.
A luminous field of an alien is found above.

The picture was taken during conversation with aliens. The essence invisible to the eye – a radiant ball of fire is fixed on the top part of a frame over Larisa Seklitova.

Photo 6. In the picture – Ludmila Strelnikova during conversation with aliens. There is a sheet with questions in front of her, which she asks space guests.

During the contact they freely hanged in any place of the room, it was fixed in the frame. In that case Edar studies home library.

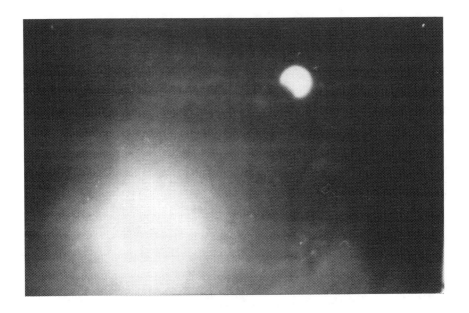

Photo 7. The picture was taken from loggia of a residential house when mini ship was flying away. It was night outside; the moon was well visible. The left lower edge is covered by a cloud. In the bottom left zone of the picture there is a luminous field of the alien ship.

Chapter 5

Aliens' visit to the cinema

After measurements of group psychophysical indicators our familiar aliens disappeared for two weeks or so. We waited for them every day, therefore our expectation was wearying, all possible fears passed through our minds: it might be something happened with them. Probably they left for ever. After all their leaders could order them to go to another planet to carry out the next task. A thought flashed also that we as primitive beings, could disappoint them, it was boring for them to communicate with us, that was why they decided not to spend any more time on us.

We suddenly felt that had time to get used to aliens and consequently started missing them and even felt sadness. Natalia came almost every day and asked whether they appeared, whether appointed the date of a new meeting.

But we did not lose time for nothing and all three together actively mastered the technique of opening the third eye. Twice a day, in the morning and in the evening, we did necessary exercises. Probably, meeting interval had been planned specially from above for us, not to rely upon someone in the person of translator, could communicate with the aliens directly.

When they suddenly appeared in our flat, Larisa and I already saw them. First saw them the daughter. She was looking out of the window when suddenly exclaimed with the muffled pleasure in her voice:

– "They have returned!"

Alexander and I rushed to the window. A small egg-shaped machine with six viewing ports hung in the air approximately 10 metres away from the house, directly at the level of our windows. The ship was silvery. It hung over the street along which cars were going and people were walking, but none of them lifted a head and were not interested in what was above. From there I concluded that they did not see this object.

Alexander, too, having fixed sight directly on the ship, asked:

– "Where are they? I, for some reason, see nobody."

– "They are here, here, straight in front of you," - emotionally said the daughter.

Alexander gathered eyebrows, tensely staring at empty azure of the fourth dimension, and judging by his face it was obvious that he saw nothing except our world. At the same time the daughter and I understood that exercises took an effect, and we saw that moment what others did not see.

Where this vision originated, it was impossible to explain, we even did not close eyes as Mr. Gromov or Dmitry did. To see the subtle world, they turned off the physical visual organ which was adjusted to see the material world, as much as possible concentrating that way on another plane. We simply saw.

The first impression was unusual. Larisa and I as if existed simultaneously in two dimensions and observed everything as it were from outside. We saw, how two planes of existence were combined, and those who were on the bottom plane, did not notice those who stayed on the top plane.

There were cars below, sparkling with multi-coloured coverings and whirring with tyres of wheels, indifferent people were walking: one – to one side, others – to the opposite. But from above all of them looked as blind men, who did not see, what occurred just over their plane of existence. It was a very strange impression, and it somehow echoed in heart with pressing melancholy. It is difficult for me to describe everything, what we saw during this short instant of enlightenment. Obviously, for completeness of the description I am just lack of concepts from other dimensions.

Alexander, however, understood at once by our fascinated faces that we saw what he did not see. But he did not take it to heart, because he was glad for us.

– "Congratulations! Lessons have not passed for nothing," - he said smiling and then joked: - "And I as a backward pupil, should repeat a year. I'll do it again."

We attentively took a good look at the silvery machine, at the windows gleaming like a mirror so that it was impossible to see something behind them. A door was not visible, it seemed, it did not exist at all.

– "Please, comment on the happening," – asked the spouse. – "otherwise guests will come and stand behind my back. And I will be still looking out of the window."

– "At last, the door has opened, the ladder is put forward," – Larisa began to describe what she was observing. – "Oh, what a long one! It has reached our loggia indeed. Very beautiful. It resembles a bridge with a handrail. Anfrida, Los, Edar are going out of the ship. Coming to us. There are here on our loggia. Have stopped."

I saw, how Anfrida, smiling, stretched out a hand through the glass to the daughter for greeting. Larisa in response held out hers, their palms touched. Both were affably smiling. Then Anfrida offered hand to me. In the place of our palms contact I felt light warmth. The same way she greeted my husband. I should take his hand and spatially put in that place where there was a hand of the girl.

After the greeting Anfrida slipped into a room through the glass and through Alexander. She passed through him as through the air, so he felt a pleasant warmth. Los and Edar followed her through the glazed loggia door.

– "It's great, we shouldn't open the door before such visitors," – said I.

– "Where have you got lost?" – Larisa asked the girl.

– "We were on the fourth continent. There was a big work. But Edar and Los were boring, because there was nobody to talk. They like to talk to different beings," - explained the alien.

– "Sit down, please," - I offered the visitors.

Los and Edar obediently sat down, Anfrida went all around room, attentively looking at household articles, she was interested in every thing. While she was examining the interior, Los addressed to us:

– "We see – you have success. Now you see and hear us. It should happen. As for the fourth continent we have not found people there who would understand us, and then have thought it would be great to have our own terrestrial translator, but, unfortunately, we understand that you are busy people, everyone has his/her business, and you cannot fly with us. Then how about you dear Alexander?" – Somehow unusually benevolently he addressed to the spouse. –"How are you doing?"

– "I am fine, thank you, nothing changed," - he sadly made a helpless gesture.

– "Do not worry. Soon it will open, too. You are a good person. We see that you work much, so it should turn out. First of all one should think that one day everything will come out. There is no impossible. You ought only to try to attain the desirable object and not to be engaged in unnecessary activity."

– "And what is «unnecessary activity»?" - He begun to worry, thinking that he was really caught in something negative, but could not understand, in what.

– "These are so-called temptations. While we were flying, we paid attention that many your people gave way to some temptations and really became stupid because of them. Many say, for example, unpleasant words. It is a temptation, too. It is not pleasant for us to listen to them. They have such a rough energy and when any low person nearby says loudly such a word …"

– "… swear," - found out Alexander.

– "Yes, that's it, swears, we are stricken with rough energy of these words, as a blast wave."

Anfrida was looking through a book with colourful pictures, but when Los said those words she turned and informed us:

– "Once I approached two young men to examine them better, but they begun to « swear » to each other so that I was knocked down by a blast wave."

– "And you, Alexander, have entered the true path, so then go and do not turn anywhere. So, you will achieve the purpose," - benevolently admonished Los.

There was a beautiful necklace made of beads on a shelf which Larisa had finished doing two days ago. Golden and white, nacreous beads in astonishing tangle of patterns were gleaming in daylight beams. The necklace awoke girl's interest, and she asked:

– "What is it? What purposes is it used for?"

– "While you were flying, I made a wally. It is put on a neck. It will match your dress very much. It is a gift specially for you. Take, please," - offered Larisa.

– "It is very beautiful. But we do not wear such. Then, we are not allowed to take something," - she casted a sidelong glance at Los. Obviously, she would like to take a gift very much.

But Los opposed at once, having caught on himself her enquiring look:

– "No, no. We have no right."

I tried to take him, as they say, at his word.

– "But you take electronics spare parts."

– "We do not take, and we make schemes. And then, it is a bad habit – to take something from other beings. We bring up Anfrida strictly. Thanks for magnanimity, but please don't present us anything. Haven't you really still understood us?"

– "Why, we perfectly understand you," - friendly assured Alexander. – "Simply earthmen have such a custom – to give another one something as a keepsake."

Edar, who loved music, always looked for a reason to listen to it once again, addressed to the daughter:

– "We have told Anfrida how you well played for us the instrument. She became interested too and would like to hear terrestrial music. Could you please play for us once again?"

– "Personally for Anfrida – I will play," - Larisa brought electro piano in a drawing-room, connected to the socket, begun to play.

Anfrida came up to Larisa and began to watch attentively her fingers. When the daughter finished, she praised:

– "Music is very good, it differs from ours. How I regret that have not studied to play."

– "Edar can teach you, if there is a desire," - answered Larisa.

– "After this flight I will necessarily take music lessons," - the alien promised. – "I will also collect, as Edar, melodies of different planets."

– "Tell, can she compose something herself?" – Los addressed Alexander.

– "Yes, she can. Last time she played one thing of own composition," - he answered.

– " thing …," - repeated bewildered Los and concluded: - "you call it incorrectly. It is called, as we have learnt, the work. Some subject is meant by the thing, and what is played and written, called not the thing."

– "People sometimes call so, though it is not absolutely correct," - Alexander began to explain. – "We often admit liberty in the language. But I beg you pardon, as I have forgotten that you require accurate and concrete concepts connected with each word."

Larisa changed her seat and sat down on a sofa. Anfrida just followed her, but when she went up to the sofa, for some reason asked:

– "Could I sit down near you?"

– "Of course."

The alien made herself comfortable nearby. At once she jumped up on it several times, as usually little children did, and delightfully exclaimed:

– "How soft it is!"

– "Do not you have the same furniture?" – Larisa was surprised.

– "No. We have only firm."

– "And on what you sleep, are your beds – soft?"

– "We have no beds."

– "What do you sleep on?"

– "People only sleep at night there, as for us, we work constantly. We only have a rest," - admitted Anfrida.

– "What way do you have a rest?" – Larisa asked again.

– "We specially come into a personal premise, and nobody will disturb us there," - the alien not so clearly explained.

When something is clear to yourself, it seems that it will be easy and clear to others. But details were required, therefore Larisa inquired:

– "Do you sit there or lie? What kind of a rest does your body need? In what pose do you prefer to have a rest?"

– "Sometimes we sit, sometimes we lie on a firm surface. Los and Edar sometimes have a rest upside-down," - and she laughed. Obviously, such a pose also looked ridiculous for her.

– "Do you have an additional charge this way?" – Alexander asked, having remembered that the man in sleep was recharged by energy.

– "This way we train for flight. There cannot be a top or a bottom in the ship when you fly in empty space, and a planet is so far. That is why we specially train in such a pose. But we have a lot of other exercises for strengthening our body. It is necessary to keep your form constantly."

– "Can you somehow during your rest enjoy youself?" – asked I. – "People have music, shows, cinemas."

– "We, too, have our own entertainments," – answered Los. It is music, as well as people have, hologram images of another worlds. We like to travel in them. There are lots of puzzles in which it is necessary to reveal secret or something to build. There are many educational and informative games. But everything is aimed at development."

– "Do you personally like to have a good time?" - I asked Los point-blank.

– "I do, only during my spare from work time. We have no right in other way. First is business, and then all the rest. But it often happens: you are so carried away by work that forget even about a rest."

– "But what exactly do you prefer in entertainments?"

– "I prefer to absorb new information, to study, how other beings live," - answered Los.

– "We have seen that you freely read our books. They are written in Russian. But there are a lot of books in other languages on the Earth. Do you speak any other language?"

– "We can read any written type. If it is unknown to us, we use a special device. It is enough to fix with it some concepts in this or that language and we can already speak it."

– "How does this device work?"

– "It translates symbols into types of energy which due to codes through quantitative and qualitative expression of this energy form semantic concept of that image contained in exact word."

– "Do you use any print on your planet to make notes?"

– "No. If you have only plane image of the information, we – only dimensional one."

– "Would Anfrida and Edar like to go to the cinema with us tomorrow?" – Larisa offered the aliens. – "Dmitry and I will go. You can look what are the ways of human entertainment."

The guests, except Los, agreed to attend an entertainment event and appointed the place and time of the meeting. Next day Larisa and Dmitry went to the cinema, but the daughter had not told him that there would be two their visitors together with them. More precisely, Dmitry did not know yet that they had returned.

There were little people at the cinema that time, the hall was almost empty. Larisa and Dmitry sat alone in the middle row. The film was wide-frame, colour.

Light faded and the screen flashed brightly. Gazes of the audience were fixed on it.

Dmitry at first was interested in film, but then felt that there was someone near them. Purely mechanically he activated the third eye and unexpectedly saw Edar who sat near Larisa, and near himself – Anfrida. But he wasn't interested in invisible girls, no matter how beautiful they were, therefore he did not pay any attention to them. But Edar's presence in an armchair near his girl-friend awfully worried the young man and didn't let him watch the film further. The plot on the screen for him stopped. Since that moment he constantly had to activate the third eye and control Edar – whether he allowed himself to go too far.

At first he was going to begin a conversation with him, but then decided that it was better to pretend that he did not see the alien. Then he would manage to reveal faster his tactless behaviour.

At the beginning Edar and Anfrida absorbed by the show, to be more exact by its analysis. Edar even came up to the screen and investigated it, then went to a light window of cinema operator in a back wall through which that man showed the film, peeped in a shining square and, having understood everything, returned to the former place.

Some time he attentively watched the screen, then it became boring for him. Obviously, another life was not so clear, and he cautiously put his big palm on Larisa's hand which lied on armrest.

Dmitry noticed it at once and was going to reprove, but decided to observe reaction of the girl.

Having felt warmth from above and having understood, what happened, she moved a hand aside. But about two minutes or so Edar again put the palm on her hand. And that time it roused Dmitry's outrage. He did not sustain and hissed, as the heated frying pan.

– "Do not use your invisibility. You should behave decently. For us such gestures are not acceptable. It is better for you to sit three rows forward. It will better watch."

– "But I don't cause something harmful," - Edar begun to protect. – "I saw the same gesture in this film. What for is it shown, if it is bad?"

– "They show to cause blame," - taught the alien a terrestrial etiquette Dmitry. – "Here one should keep away from girls."

On the one hand, he would like to look before the representative of another planet a hospitable owner, but, on the other hand, something in him prevented to that, and when he saw Edar sitting close to his girl-friend, he turned to the quarrelsome old man.

Both girls watched the film with an interest without paying attention to Dmitry's morals. When the film ended, Larisa addressed the alien:

– "How do you like our entertainment? Was everything clear?"

– "Behaviour of people was not clear," - admitted Anfrida. – "you have your own subtleties of mutual relations, which are absent at our end. But if to speak about creation technology it was very amusing for me to look at the plane person. In life I see the man dimensionally with a shining field around. And the person on the screen is a moving scheme. There is neither aura, nor subtle structures. Your know-how is not yet capable to display them. The plane person is very funny, it reminds the drawn on a paper. I saw such on your wall."

– "And what will you tell concerning the seen?" - Larisa turned towards Edar. – "Does the plane image seem to you strange, too?"

– "Yes, for me they were also paper little men. But I understood that they are made basing on the play of light and darkness. They create various tints and shades, and this shade already runs on your wall. It turns out very funny. But we say thank you that you have invited us to such show. We would not see it ourselves, as took a cinema for your following station."

It was interesting to Larisa to hear their opinion about what is not present on their planet, to hear an unusual point of view among usual everyday estimations of the human, and for the sake of it she had invited them to watch movie though expected that it would produce a big impression on them.

Right after the end of the film aliens flew away on the mini-ship to the basic multiprobe which was hundreds kilometers away from us. They promised to come once again to a session of the group. However, they also pursued their aims there – decided by common consent of interested persons to make some additional measurements.

The meeting took place in appointed time. Only two men allowed taking from them measurements. Others, being afraid of that it could cause harm, refused.

– "Please, read out our previous indicators," - declared Michael.

– "They will be not clear to you," - Los evaded the question.

– "Well, well! What for, then, to take new if we do not know previous," - objected Michael.

– "And do you know the structure of your subtle bodies?" - asked him Los.

– "We know only that they exist. For us it is a foggy cloud," - our materialist melancholically admitted.

– "We tried to find in your literature any information about subtle bodies, but found nothing," - I explained our ignorance.

– "I ask it because indicators are just connected with a structure of your subtle bodies, and if you do not know it, how can we explain what is unknown to you," – Los tried to give reasons for the refusal to announce psycho-physical data.

Natalia cunningly looked at Michael and whispered:

– "They are, likely, so low in comparison with them that they are ashamed to speak about it. We lagged behind them for one thousand years if not more."

– "Do you have any questions to the aliens?" – I addressed the group.

– "Please, ask. We will add while we are about it," - answered Mr.Gromov.

Taking a sheet with prepared questions, I entered the conversation with newcomers.

– "Do different beings exist on your planet? For example, people differ by the nations. There are three races: black, white and yellow. What distinctions do you have between your beings?"

– "There are no special distinctions. We are all alike and also of one colour. Beings differ only in development level. The more a being lives, the cleverer he is, as he manages to learn more information."

– "You, probably, have noticed that people live in different countries. We have also different social orders on the Earth. Is there on your planet a division into the countries?"

– "No. Our beings live together in one country. There is no division between our beings. We are surprised, why do people separate from each other? Don't they know, that separation and isolation lead to degradation? All of us consider ourselves as one big family and are very respectfully disposed to each other."

– "Don't your beings really have disputes, insults, disagreements?"

– "There can be different points of view on one issue. But we respect opinion of everyone because every being has a right to it. What for - to argue? You shouldn't force your ideas upon other being because his soul is constructed in another way and produces own point of view on everything," - explained Los.

– "You are right," - agreed I. – "as for us, it's the other way round, some people try to force one idea to millions."

– "Never mind, time will pass, and the person, too, will understand everything, there will be one united state on the Earth."

– "You freely fly in space. In our films people are frightened by presence in Space some snarks. Do they really live somewhere? Have you met them?" – I was curious.

– "Snarks – do you mean monsters?" – asked again Edar.

– "Yes."

– "In our plane of existence we haven't met such forms. But we know that one can meet terrible beings sometimes on the bottom planes. However, they cannot get into your world, and furthermore – in ours as we stand by Level above people. Alhough there are pirates in Space. They live on some planets. These are beings – parasites. They do not wish to do something, and use everything prepared."

– "Did you personally meet them?" – asked Mr.Gromov.

– "Yes, several times we were to meet them. But we flew away from them at high speed."

– "Can you only take refuge in flight?" – asked I.

– "No. We often use energy protection – we cover our ship with a special field which makes it invisible to other beings. We suddenly disappear for them, and they think that we have gone away, and come back."

– "When a ship suddenly drops out of sight, is it always covered with such a field?" – asked Alexander.

– "Not necessarily. Sometimes it picks up high speed, and if a being has a slowed-down reaction, as the human has, it seems to him/her that a ship has disappeared. It is simply his visual organ which is not capable to catch a chain of consecutive stages of device movement. Besides, it happens that a ship moves into another dimension. Do you yourself understand, what people are very slow-moving?" – Edar addressed to members of the group.

– "Not a bit of it, of course, no. We seem ourselves quick as mice," - joked Natalia.

– "Yes, it can be understood only in comparison with others," - noticed Los.

– "Do you know, why has the person such a short life?" – I asked the next question. – "as far as we know, the majority of beings surpass the person in duration of existence many times. You, for example, live for more than thousand years."

– "Yes, why is it so unfair?" –at once roused herself Natalia. – "We live fifty years, and others – millions. What has God got against us?"

– "Insufficient consciousness and tendency to fall into temptations disturb you," - answered Los. – "the person himself either extends the life, or shortens it."

Meanwhile Anfrida was working with volunteers, taking some measurements.

– "I have not understood," - declared Mr.Gromov. – "what is the connection between my consciousness and span of life?"

– "Low beings are not capable to long development," - began to explain Los. – "They can live normally only short intervals and then are put on the spot. During their first years of life they perceive something, study and then stop in their development and begin degrading. Sometimes degradation can be so powerful that it destroys everything what a being has got before. It turns out that their life passes for nothing, all successes turn into minus. They are not capable to be interested in something for a long time. The life itself becomes boring to them. And to prevent degradation, they are taken from life earlier, before the moment when it can occur. Nevertheless it is more often when degradation happens, and it ceases by way of life interruption. In such a way they are not allowed to destroy themselves, to degrade. But at the same time the sum of several short lives gives to soul good accumulation."

– "But why do they start to degrade? In what is it shown up?" – I began trying to worm out the core of the case.

– "They do not know the purpose of existence, for what they have come to this world, give way to temptations. They take temptations for the value of life and start to aspire constantly to them," - continued to explain Los.

– "How it resembles people," - agreed I. An enlightenment unexpectedly came to us. – "then, probably, death in wars on the Earth of many young men is the cessation of their development to prevent further degradation, isn't it?"

– "Probably," - agreed Los. – "But the human conducts wars himself because of own aggression. We do not understand, why people are such aggressive, why do they badly disposed to us, aliens?"

At that time I could not answer the question yet. Edar shared his observations, adding to words of Los:

– "They also are afraid of invisible beings, though they are no more harmful to them, than the air. The person first starts to shoot before greeting. That's a good thing the bullet passes through them without harm."

I had nothing to say for people, therefore I decided to change unpleasant topic.

– "What way does consciousness prolong the life?"

– "A being with high consciousness correctly chooses the development purpose, makes less mistakes, therefore it is allowed to exist longer. The most important thing is not to make mistakes."

– "Tell us please, are there animals on your planet?" - I addressed to Los.

– "No. They are not necessary for us. These are your souls, which go from the form of animals to the form of the man, and as for us, our souls develop in one form for a long time."

– "And then where do your souls go to?"

– "To other planets … But why do others keep silence?" – asked Los. – "What can you tell us about yourselves? What plans do you have for the future?"

– "Mr.Gromov and I are going to enter Avdeev's «School of phantoms»," - Michael shared the plans. – "Have you heard about this school?"

– "No."

– "This school teaches how to become the same, as you. We will learn to leave the physical body and so can meet you in an etheric body."

– "We approve your intentions," - solemnly said Los. – "If you become the same as we, it will be possible to invite you to the ship. So try."

– "It is a stimulus for us," - Michael was delighted.

– "But I notify: you should study intensively, otherwise you can be late. We will carry through with the business and fly away."

After such warning Michael and Mr.Gromov there and then went to Moscow «School of phantoms», organized by Mr.Avdeev, who was a parapsychologist, philosopher and spoke aphoristically and non-standard. We, however, stayed at home. Larisa declared that she had understood how to leave the body, and all of us decided to dare what would turn out. The persistence on the way of a set goals attainment fastens its achievement.

One day we three together sat in daughter's room and did the first exercises. Suddenly we saw, how the wire with a plug from the electro piano rose over the instrument, floated to a wall and was thrusted into the socket, after that keys as though itself began to play unfamiliar melody. We looked with surprise how keys quickly jumped upwards, downwards, one after another, deriving sounds. But music was obviously of the space origin.

«Edar», – we understood. It was he who decided to play a trick on us. We caught an appropriate wave and really saw Edar standing at the instrument and playing one of the melodies. Near him there were Anfrida and Los. Both smiling.

– "We decided to make a small miracle," - admitted Anfrida. – "How do you like it?"

– "Very much," - answered Larisa. – "you know, it is very interesting to look at the piano playing in different ranges of frequencies. In a material world only keys play, and in subtle one – a handsome stranger."

– "Do you really think that I am handsome?" – Edar was even confused from such praise. – "or is it a joke?"

– " It is an allegoric expression," – Larisa explained, but not to hurt him added then:

– "But you completely correspond to this comparison. You all have beautiful souls, and infinite possibilities for their revealing in our world. There are not enough such courageous and resolute beings among people," – she diplomatically turned from compliments to one alien to a praise of everybody, and it touched them very much.

– "Nobody has told us such a good words for a long time," - said touched Los. – "Thank you very much for your kind attitude to us. Do you know, where have we just arrived to you from?"

– "No," - Larisa shook a head.

– "We have arrived from the Moon."

– "Do you fly to the Moon?" – Alexander was surprised.

– "Yes. By the way, we have friends there too," - informed Edar.

– "Are there any living beings on the Moon?" – doubted I.

– "In the physical plane you will see nobody, and in the subtle world reasonable beings live there, too, and at the same time there are several forms of them. There are, too, buildings and equipment. Haven't you really known about it?"

– "No," - I had to admit again our lack of information. But simultaneously a thought flashed through my mind: it might be that «aliens play us?», therefore to check them I asked:

– "Describe us please these lunar inhabitants. We have no idea about them."

– "What for should we describe them? You can see them yourselves. Would you like to get acquainted with them?" - unexpectedly offered Edar. – "You live nearby and do not know each other."

– "Is it really possible?" – hesitantly said I. It seemed to me that the joke went on.

– "Of course it is possible," - nodded he. – "We can bring Larisa on our ship to the Moon if she, of course, wants."

His offer was tempting.

– "How is it, in a physical body?" – Alexander asked again.

– "No. In subtle one. We can much. Your companions have gone to study, and let they study, so we can help you, more precisely, Larisa. She has more makings for this purpose. We shall open for her the exit channel out of the body, but only for a while. Then we shall close it, as we have no right to break your program."

– "But it is, likely, dangerous," - I begun to worry. First, daughter's going out of the body was terrible and, secondly, it was terrible to let her go with strange beings to unexplored space distances. «If they suddenly take away and leave for themselves. Second Anfrida» will turn out," - flashed through my mind, and I asked aloud: - "Will it cause no harm to her health?"

– "Certainly. Though for your bodies we have higher pressure on the ship, but we shall cover her with a protective field. Everything will be ok. We have a sense of responsibility. We promise that nothing will happen to her," - persuaded Edar.

Anfrida joined him.

– "Do not worry. I take her under my wing. It will be pleasure for me to make even one flight with a being, precisely the same, as I. Do you think, that it takes much time to fly to the Moon? Only some minutes are for our ship. In your standards we will be absent no more than two hours," - she promised.

The daughter, of course, had a violent urge to go.

– "I am ready to fly with you," - she agreed, and there was no even slightest hesitation in her voice.

Certainly, the offer was tempting and simultaneously dangerous. Doubts overwhelmed me as the mother, but they did not flash in daughter's eyes even for a minute. The decision was already made, and I needed only to agree with it.

– "But what if she suddenly feels bad?" – assumed I. – "After all she hasn't trained to become a cosmonaut."

– "It is more difficult in a physical body. But in subtle – is easier, less gravity loads," - explained Anfrida. – "Moreover, it is not far away. It's all the same as if, in your standards, to go by bus one stop."

– "When shall we leave? I shall definitely fly," - Larisa promised, and to talk her out of going was useless.

– "Tomorrow. We shall inform you when to wait for us. We shall bring them something and meanwhile take Larisa for a drive," - promised Los. – "Get in good with us, we'll be good to you."

– "Is it possible for me too?" – asked I. – "Together it would be more cheerful."

– "We are afraid that if you leave your body, you will not come back. There are small damages in your construction. We cannot risk you. Do not worry about Larisa, everything will be tip-top. Protection in the ship is excellent, we have tested it on ourselves more than once," - assured Edar.

– "Ok, we shall think till tomorrow," - answered I. As for them, not staying any more, they left the room.

We did not try to talk the daughter out of it. Belief in decency of our acquaintances took roots in us all the same. «If they promise, it means they will do it», decided we. Having discussed unexpected offer, we began to wait for next day with impatience. We were so carried away with all new in knowledge that no dangers could serve as an obstacle. How much I would like to dash away together with them to star heights and to dissolve in boundless spaciousness of the Universe! But for a while one of us had the good fortune, and we should be happy that the sacrament touched us.

Chapter 6

Flight to the Moon

Spaceship of aliens hung highly in the sky. Anfrida and Edar flew up to the house on the mini-ship and stopped near the loggia. Both entered the room where we were waiting for them. Edar praised us:

– "I see in your auras readiness number one. All of you are ready to fly. It is good. But only the youngest member of your community flies. You can now observe Larisa," - Edar addressed me. – "First of all she will fly out «of herself», and then blast off from Earth.

The daughter sat down in an armchair. «First step» separation began, i.e. from physical body. She began as though to split in two. Soon one daughter stayed sitting in the room as if sleeping, another, radiant, stopped near an armchair and calmed us:

– "It's all right. Do not worry. I feel so easy. As if I have just thrown down one pood weight from my feet."

Edar paid the daughter a compliment:

– "In a subtle body you are more beautiful, than in material. The hugest range of radiations. We judge the beauty of the person by radiations."

– "Now regarding you from a detached spirit I see that material body as a plaster bag, holds down. I even breath easier. Although it is self-deception …" - at once she took herself at her word. – "I have no lungs right now."

– "Let's not waste time," - said Anfrida and, taking the daughter by the hand, went to the mini-ship.

Both freely passed through the closed balcony door, and I thought: «Now she can pass through walls. Likely, this is an amusing feeling».

Before entering the ship, both girls turned and waved their hands to us. Then they came into the ship. Edar followed them. The sliding door closed, the ship soared upwards. We began waiting.

Here I will make a digression, telling about my past experience.

While they were flying, I recollected the meeting with other aliens, happened in my youth. That, what you take sometimes for a dream or simply for something not clear and mysterious, happened with you earlier, one day you reveal a new side of it. Probably, every man has some strangeness in his/her life, which he/she cannot give the answer at once and even is not capable to understand – has it been in reality or is it only a mirage. Much time has passed before a searching consciousness finds the answer. But, I stress, only the one who looks for – will find.

When I was young, twenty years old, and lived two thousand kilometers away from this place, once, having woken up at night, I felt that my body was held down, I could not stir neither a hand, nor a foot. A thought flashed through my mind: «Is it really the paralysis made me moveless? In twenty years and it's a paralysis! But I have been absolutely healthy». And as if replying to the thoughts suddenly someone's powerful and calm voice appeared in my mind. I heard the orders given by it in myself clearly, and for some reason I understood that had no right to disobey and should perform accurately what it would tell me.

– "Three waves will go now. You should bear. Be ready. It is necessary to sustain."

I understood that I was woken specially because those unpleasant sensations which they sent to me, I should apprehend with full consciousness, mobilize all my strength of will to sustain. Those who gave orders had made me motionless. It was a preventive measure in case if I had spoiled their work with some gesture.

I began waiting. The voice in my mind sounded again.

– "The first wave has gone."

What it was the sensation! I was as if flattened, pressed down by something extremely heavy and not to be crushed to a clot, I should brace the muscles very much to withstand this pressure. Besides, there was such a vibration as though I laid on a pickhammer, which helped to break off pieces of an old asphalt. Vibrations were small, but surprisingly offensive.

Minutes for me turned to eternity, because it was very difficult to sustain these vibrations, and each second of unpleasant sensations was stretched in consciousness for extremely long term. At last, vibration came to an end. The first wave passed.

They allowed me to have a rest for some seconds, then I heard the voice again:

– "The second wave has gone."

It was heavy too. And I looked forward, when the third wave, the last, would come and everything would be over. I even began to feel arrival of that invisible wave without any notification, I as if felt it with the sixth sense. The wave had only come out its mysterious source, and I already felt it. The wave came, I met it with a strain of all my internal force. I would have felt the same if I, likely, had lifted 50 kilogram bag.

At last, the third wave ended. They ordered me:

– "Sleep," - and I fell asleep.

Next morning I woke up vigorous and healthy. No trace remained from "paralysis". But I remembered everything and memory remained for a whole life. What was it? Why did I so obediently carry out their orders? And where did I know from, that I had no right to disobey? The soul knew that those were the Higher and that I should obey Them, knew that there was nobody to be afraid of. There was no fear at all. But where did that knowledge come from? Why did I hear them inside, without hearing a sound voice?

Many questions arose then in my mind, but it was not possible to find even one answer during that time, because there was no information about aliens. If there was some data, it belonged to the category of fantasy or was hidden from the majority.

The second meeting with these not clear orders and waves happened in a month. They woke me again at night, it was the same voice:

– "Waves will come. Be ready."

That time they did not tell how many waves it would be, but I already knew that there would be three. Those waves were a bit easier, though also caused very unpleasant sensations. It seemed, not clear vibration penetrated each cell of the body. Waves came and left. Nothing more.

But a week later someone appeared in a room. I could not perceive him with a physical vision, but felt with the sixth sense. I also woke up at night, obviously, he woke me for conversation, and I was laying under a blanket up to my chin. I understood that someone had appeared in a room, and knew, where he stood. The invisible stranger asked:

– "How's your health?"

– "All right."

We talked mentally.

– "Would you like, I shall take you away with me?"

To his offer a curious question flashed at once. I was not going to leave somewhere, but I was just interested: how would he take me away, if there was the roof above us. And I for some reason knew, that we should rise through it. But that time I had no idea of how the physical body could be left, and how to fly in other subtle bodies. I was interested in methods of rising, therefore, before telling "No", I curiously asked:

– "But how is it possible to fly through the roof upwards?"

The invisible being as though grinned, made smooth hand gesture upwards as if lifted someone in the sky, and said:

– "I will pick you up."

– "No. I cannot. People need me," - I refused the invitation. That day the soul for some reason knew life goals. But to achieve them, it should pass thirty three more difficult years.

Only now I understand that it has been my testing. I was offered to avoid thirty three-year way of sufferings and return to the Higher Brothers. But I felt the duty before younger brothers and that was why stayed on the Earth.

This soul sense of the program is very important: it is important to learn to feel the duty and to distinguish it from your desires. Certainly, I had a desire to leave everything and go away from there forever. However the duty outweighed.

But the riddle remained. I cannot understand till now what they did with those waves: took some individual measures, fixed additional subtle constructions or, just in case, made a copy of me, i.e. a copy from construction of a physical body and three temporary subtle ones. I have not found answers to these questions. I shall know about it just after my death.

The only thing I know that there haven't been the same aliens, as Edar and Los. Those were Heads. As for Edar and Los they were ordinary space workers, as our cosmonauts. But communication with beings from the planet 327, if it is possible to say on equal terms, helped us to master other dimensions, to cross borders of the worlds and to find something common between them.

And that day Larisa, too, crossed the border of two different, but adjacent worlds, it was her first acquaintance with another world. By the way, I remembered that daughter, too, was twenty years old. Hence, the meeting with Edar and Los was planned for us.

It was a riddle for me some time ago, how did They find a certain person among millions? But then decided that chips were installed in our biostructure, so they sent a message regarding our current location. The point was that my first meeting with aliens took place in Novorossiysk city. That time I was a student. Then I was transferred to another institute in Rostov-on-Don (obviously for a meeting with my future husband), lived there with one old woman, but aliens found me and there.

They conducted the last, control test. Also at night I woke up knowing that three waves would come, and I should sustain. That time waves were weak, and I sustained them easily enough.

When waves had ended, I heard:

– "Good-bye. So now we are meeting in the end of your way."

There I first asked a question, how could they find me? They kept an eye on me during a year or so.

Besides, I would like to tell about one more meeting with beings from another planet. I quote this story as an example of various meetings with representatives of other worlds. I also would like to show, how differently these meetings can be held: someone can arrive to you, or sometimes you can "arrive" to other worlds. Larisa, for example, went away with the help of other aliens, and I flew with the help of my Heavenly Teacher. At the time I was already married, Larisa was around seven, we lived in Al-va, where, by the way, our main channelings begun.

At night I opened my eyes because someone woke me and informed:

– "You will go to another planet. Be ready, close your eyes."

For some reason I understood at once that my Teacher spoke. The impression of his voice was as though the announcer was speaking off screen and I was the main character in that film. Unlike the first aliens who sent me waves, the voice was more talkative. It managed me, ordering:

–"Please, concentrate. You are flying."

And I rushed at such unusual speed that it seemed to me, that the wind was shrilly whistling, I rapidly cut through some environment and it made me sense that whistle. There were neither stars around, nor the usual sky, only some not clear grey haze as if I flew in the fog.

– "Brake," - ordered the voice.

I felt that had made incredible efforts to brake, and became aware of how difficult to concentrate your power inside.

– "Turn right," - continued to order the voice.

There was a planet then. I landed in some settlement where there were only one-storeyed small houses. Red walls of around six metres height towered in the middle of a small town. They made some ominous impression. The district resembled our Northern Caucasus foothills belt. But I felt clearly that the planet was strange to me, that everything there was alien: the greenish sky, a poor nature, white square small houses with flat roofs.

I was a little aside from a small town on some hill, dense high bushes grew nearby. Most of all my attention was focused on a red wall. I could see what was behind it.

– "Be attentive," - the voice announced off-screen and warned: - "Not to be noticed, hide in a shade and do not move, whatever you will see."

I came into a shade of high bushes and began waiting for further events. Inhabitants appeared in a small town. Obviously, their work was finished, and they went home.

Something evil appeared in atmosphere. It quickly increased. There were reddish gleams in the sky, then after that bald creatures, looked like people, began to fly out of the red wall. They freely were floating in the air as hawks looking out for quarry below. Then they rushed to the crowd, snatched a man and as soon as he appeared in their hands both became invisible. But I knew that they carried away people behind the wall.

A terrible panic arose below. Everybody ran, begun to cry. As for the bald they snatched one after another and as soap bubbles, burst in the air, dropping out of sight.

When the last bald with his victim disappeared, silence and quietness reigned in the town. As if people forgot everything at once. And it was that what amazed me most of all. Why was such a contrast in their behaviour? There had been hysterically rushing about and shouting people before, and in a minute were again, so quiet and indifferent, as if nothing had happened, and there were no losses among them.

I drew an analogy with hens running and cackling, when a kite snatched one of them and when it flew away, they became quiet and, peacefully pacing up and down, tried to find kernels. Either there is any protection in consciousness of beings with such way of life, or low development of their consciousness does not allow estimating completely the spirit of tragedy, happened with their, let me say, relatives.

Thus, since then I cannot simply tolerate the bald (only those who shaves themselves). I never knew what were those beings and what they did with people, i.e. the beings alike us. But after fifteen years or so I saw a fantastic film of one director about bald flying aliens who chased people just on our planet, and was surprised with accuracy of their appearance and a behaviour manner, all coincided with what I had seen.

There were the same flying bald, with the same habits. But now from the film I knew that they took people to investigate their souls. I understood that this director had received the information from the Teacher about the same beings, or, probably, flew there himself.

It was a meeting with minus beings. Thus, I had to learn feeling their soul, to remember some their characteristic features, so to see them in others similar to them. External forms vary, but the essence of the minus remains invariable, and it becomes more and more while developing.

But the first open experience of a meeting with minus beings was the brightest. Among the details noticed by consciousness the most well-defined for me remained: bald heads and an ominously-red wall. One should know how to distinguish the evil before its starting to show up.

By the way, later on I noticed several times that those people who had hair, but specially shaved completely, often showed themselves from a negative side. It turned out that a person had behaved adequately for a long time, but then played such a prank that you were surprised how could he reveal such meanness or cruelty. Probably, it slumbers up to a certain time and once wakes up.

In this case I have made the reader aware of my past experience of different contacts. The first were the aliens arriving to our Earth for work under God's orders. They remained invisible to us only because they were in other dimension. And they were highly-developed in comparison with people. The second (the bald and their victims) referred to material beings. Each of them conducted own way of life: one (the bald) – minus one, others (their victims) – plus one. The first were spiritually high, the second – very low. It is the soul which should define the difference.

– – –

However, let's return, as they say, by now, by the present moment. Here, using Larisa's story, I shall describe everything what has happened with them.

The mini-ship, which the daughter with our familiar aliens boarded, quickly reached the multiprobe and entered a reception module. The passenger and crewmen left it and came into a spacious room of silvery-bluish colour. There were some devices with luminous screens and pointers on one side, and cupboards on the other side.

–"This is our working room," - declared Anfrida. – "Everything is automatic here, it works from buttons." – to prove it she began to press buttons.

A round table with two chairs rose directly out of the floor. Everything was firm, as the alien had told. The girl pressed the button on a wall, and the bed, i.e. simply flat surface pulled out from there.

– "One can have a rest here," - explained Anfrida. – "We also have armchairs, which move. Look," – she pressed one more button, and from another room a vacant armchair came. – "Sit down," - offered she. Larisa sat down, the armchair began to drive about with her around the

premise, and then went up to the alien and stopped. Larisa stood up.
—"Sometimes I drive in it," - admitted Anfrida. – "But it is convenient also for transportations of something." – then Anfrida came up to a back wall and having pressed the buttons, opened small rooms, which Larisa had taken for closed cupboards. "These are subsidiary rooms for our needs," - declared the alien.

– "Do you really have them?" – a little confusedly asked Larisa.

Anfrida laughed:

– "You, people, are strange. Don't you really think, that we need nothing? We have everything on the ship, up to the shower, so you can be purified."

The girl pressed some more buttons and some other not clear devices came up out of walls, but the Earthwoman was not so interested in them.

After visiting all the premises Larisa went up to a window to admire the star sky and to look at the Earth at a distance, but only a black haze was spread out behind the glass. Neither a little star, nor any planet was not visible.

Edar came up and having understood her bewilderment explained:

– "Do not forget that you are in the subtle world. All physical objects disappeared from a field of vision. Here it is the other world and other structure. Besides, your visual organ works in a slowed-down way, and as we fly with such a speed, you will have no time to distinguish anything with your terrestrial construction. I can show you our devices," - he offered and brought her up to the wall with rows of all possible devices which maintained order inside the ship.

Larisa attentively looked closely at them, but they seemed to her not clear, however, understanding that they were among Edar's favourite things praised:

– "Very interesting devices, accurate, beautiful and, likely, they are so durable that there is no need to repair."

– "Los and I have made some devices ourselves," - boasted Edar. – "We can do much." – "and changing the topic from equipment to lyrics, he musefully said: - "How it would be good, if you stayed on our ship. A new colleague would treble my power. Anfrida would have a new companion, and I – the friend. How many new melodies I would have composed then!" – but, having seen an indulgent smile on the face of the Earthwoman, corrected himself: – "Of course, I understand that now it is impossible. But only now. Everything changes in due course. I can wait eternally."

Los appeared from another module.

– "I welcome the first inhabitant of the Earth on our ship," - smiled he.

Larisa addressed to him:

– "You have one more crewman, haven't you?"

– "He steers the ship. Fit is the genuine captain of the Space," - praised him Los, - "he is able to extricate the ship from difficult situations. How do you like our machine?"

– "Splendid. It produces a big impression," - the Earth woman praised, despite had no time to examine it all. She was going to continue survey, but Anfrida informed:

– "Have landed on the Moon in the second parallel world."

We arrived very quickly. The impression was that it took no more than twenty minutes for flight.

We landed near some Lunar city. There were high-risers far away. The city was small, but looked super-modern. There were no one-storeyed constructions there.

The lunar landscape did not tally with that, which was known to the man from photos of scientists. There were neither dust, nor churned up soils from the falling meteorites, no craters and no hollows. The sky was shining with yellowish colour, the surface underfoot looked smooth and clean. There wasn't any mountain within of eyeshot.

Edar, having noticed, how the Earth woman was watching a surrounding space, understood her:

– "Are you comparing with a material world? You are aware of the first world, we are in the second. They are so much different, as your material body and subtle one. If you tell terrestrial scientists what you have seen, they will not believe, because you look at different worlds, although they belong to one object. A problem of the person is that he/she is not capable to see different dimensions. Therefore, when he/she is told about the parallel world, he/she considers that it is a delirium of sick imagination. And each world tries to adapt what he/she sees with material eyes and can sense."

– "Are you familiar with works of our scientists?" – Larisa smiled, hinting that, aliens liked to investigate innovations of others. But Edar did not pay attention to that hint.

– "Yes, we keep an eye on their researches. But as for machinery or understanding of other worlds, they lag many steps behind us. They should join knowledge of the material and subtle worlds."

As soon as four of them left the ship and walked on the Moon surface, a small group of lunar inhabitants went towards.

Walking on the moon surface, Larisa paid attention that her soles were heated, it became hot, and she could not explain why.

– "It is somehow hot to my feet," - she looked downwards, trying to find there the reason.

– "We shall turn on protection. The person perceives a very small range of temperatures," - explained Anfrida and, having pressed the button in a small round device, put it into Larisa's pocket. Sensations became normal.

Lunar inhabitants came soon. There were five adults and three little, obviously, children among them.

Appearance of lunarmen differed both from the person, and from the aliens. They were not high, so their maximum height was one and a half metre. Edar was half-metre higher. Los and Anfrida had the height of the average person. The body of lunar inhabitants looked similar to human except for little details.

All the difference was focused on the head. It reminded egg. Lunar inhabitants had no hair at all. Ears were like big burdocks, eyes were small, round. The mouth reminded a mouth of our wooden dolls-puppets. During conversation their lower lip went down, and the upper one remained motionless.

The most remarkable they had a nose. It was like children's pipe which began from the face with the narrow end and getting further from it extended in a form of funnel. The nose, obviously, was sensitive because funnel edges slightly moved all the time: trembled, got narrower, inhaled or again widened.

Lunarmen joyfully welcomed their good friends and welcomed them in a special way: stretched their hands wide, embraced aliens who, because of their superiority in height, had to bow, then came back, as though looking over the one, whom they greeted, from head to foot, then again went up to and embraced. And so three times one after another.

Having finished greeting ritual, they stopped in front of the stranger. They saw the girl with magnificent white hair for the first time, so confusedly looked at her, not knowing how to begin.

Larisa welcomed them in her own terrestrial way, offering a hand to one of them.

– "Hello."

But at once they shook their heads:

– "It is not accepted here. We give hugs."

Edar came to the rescue of her.

–"She is a guest from the Earth. She is here for the first time. When she gets used to you, will greet the same way."

Los got into a car, which looked like a big ladybird, and left with two lunar representatives. The car dashed away rapidly to the lunar airport, which was located on the left of the lunar landing place. The building had a monumental character and was with a big transparent dome instead of a roof usual for us. Nearby there were some flying machines, which looked like big dirigibles with windows. There were also small, reminding "plates" covered above with glass caps. All ships by their form were known to terrestrial researchers of unidentified flying objects. She did not see anything new there.

– "Do you like lunar landscape?" – asked Anfrida. – "It is simpler than the terrestrial."

– "Yes, I like it. Despite it is similar to ours, I feel for some reason its strangeness, for me it looks alien. Even some strange chill creeps into heart," - answered Larisa.

– "It always happens, when you arrive to a strange world. The soul feels that your body is created from another matter. You are created from a terrestrial one, therefore the soul does not accept another. But this feeling appears only during the first moments, then you get used," - explained Anfrida.

– "There is so powerful civilization on the Moon, but people consider that it is empty," - the Earth woman said thoughtfully.

– "It is the next delusion of the person," - smiled Edar. – "First he forms for himself a wrong notion of something and when it is shattered, he is frightened. For example, the man has the idea that there is nobody in Space except him and when other beings appear, he dies from fear. It is ridiculous."

– "Yes, but there's nothing to be done. It takes some time to prove him that there are lots of living forms around," -answered Larisa.

– "By the way, do you know, what is the difference between the Moon and the Earth?" – asked Edar.

Lunar inhabitants stood near him and, as they say, "stared" at the being new to them. They laughed for some reason when Edar asked that question.

No doubt, Larisa did not know this difference, but tried to assume.

– "There is no nature on the Moon."

– "It is so. But the main difference is that the Moon - is artificial, and the Earth – alive."

– "People do not know it," - the Earth woman admitted.

One of lunar inhabitants, wishing to put wise a being from the Earth, began to explain:

– "Each world of one planet can easily, without translators, come in contact with a similar world on the other planet: material – with material, etheric – with etheric or close to it and so on, using telepathy. But if they try the other way round, it will turn out nothing, because each being adapts to the world."

Larisa paid attention that they were also dressed in fitting overalls. It seemed to her that overalls is universal clothes for the etheric world, therefore she asked:

– "Don't you wear other clothes?"

– "No. It is convenient."

– "And people spend a lot of time for creation of different clothes," - noticed Anfrida. – "But I like some it's forms," – at the same time she was still in a red dress.

– "If you want, I will present you some dresses," –offered Larisa. – "I sew myself, so for me it is not a problem."

– "I do not know," - vaguely answered Anfrida. But as any young soul, she was tortured by temptation.

– "Larisa is Jack of all trades," - praised her Edar.

– "But don't you feel cold or vice versa hot in your clothes?" – The daughter addressed lunarmen.

– "No. Our clothes is capable to regulate temperature drops. This is its main advantage," - one of the present answered. – "we consider it is inexpedient to waste time on clothes, but we sometimes change colours. What are your occupations on the Earth?" – he was curious.

– "We have a club where we with a group of enthusiasts gather and investigate life of other beings, unusual phenomena," - the daughter answered with dignity, wishing to show that people were not so know-nothing in studying of that was beyond the bounds of visibility. – "We even carry out experiments sometimes. There are people with different abilities in our group."

– "Can we come to you?" – One of lunar inhabitants unexpectedly wangled an invitation. – "As we have got acquainted and you see that we are not terrible and not malicious it would be good getting to know each other better. You and we have such possibility not often," – persuaded he.

– "But how will you get to us?" - The daughter hesitated.

– "Edar will take us the same as you," - declared the lunarman.

– "If so, please. You are welcome," - agreed the daughter.

She came back excited, full of impressions. The mini-ship brought her up to the loggia. And she returned to the room. However, temporarily she lost bearings, it might be because of flight, or emotions overwhelming her. She had to reunite with the body, but she lost it. Visibility of the material world became dark. She saw everything hazily. She had no particular experience to distinguish material objects from the subtle world. But Edar and Anfrida did not want to show it.

Larisa came up to the father, but felt that it wasn't her form; came up to me and sensed that that was another too. At last, approached to the body and by some general interactions of fields understood that found what had looked for.

Edar and Anfrida took her wandering around the room for granted, having decided that she simply did a greeting ritual. When the daughter came up to the body, they helped to reunite with it and warned, not to try leaving, as it was forbidden. Who and why forbade, they did not say. They also exhorted that it would be better to tell about that flight nobody, as everything would be misunderstood.

However, Edar asked with an interest about daughter's impression got from traveling:

– "How's the flight? Did you like it?"

– " It's never-to-be-forgotten. I shall remember it till the end of my life. It would like to repeat."

– "Unfortunately, I cannot any more. I broke all bans which were put. They can punish me for it."

– "What are bans put?" – The daughter was surprised.

– "Don't you know about it?" - naively asked Edar.

– "No."

– "All members of your family have special Higher signs in subtle plane on your bodies. In accordance with the space symbolics we know that these beings have inviolability. No one from other worlds has right to cause such beings damage or to involve in risky situations. And I have brought you to the Moon, flight is a big risk. But I would like to make you happy. I cannot present anything, only give you pleasure. Basing on my own experience I know that there is nothing more lively than flight and meeting with friends."

– "Thank you. For me, it was really the best travel in my life. I think, you have done properly. To see absolutely different world is a new experience for the soul ..." - she hesitated, not daring to ask something, then made up her mind: - "Don't you know, who has signed us?"

Edar shook a head.

– "Nobody among beings knows. But it is well-known to us that those, who caused harm to beings with signs, were severely punished and even turned into slaves."

After some more insignificant phrases exchange and having left us to share impressions, aliens flew away.

The daughter began to tell in details about her trip. When she reached the moment when lunar inhabitants wangled an invitation, Alexander said jokingly:

– "Now, it is the same as with Ostap Bender, our city turns into New-Vasjuki, the centre of general universal meetings and contacts. They have had an interstellar chess tournament, and we shall have an interplanetary symposium. We shall hold a symposium on forging relationships with different worlds."

Despite he spoke playfully, his eyes burnt with inspiration. We began to wait for new visitors with impatience.

Here I wish to notice that neither Larisa, nor anybody else of us hadn't seen lunar inhabitants before. Nobody knew what form did they have. To imagine them better, the daughter drew them on a sheet of paper. But three months later we watched on TV an American cartoon about an alien and suddenly recognized out lunarmen. The alien had the same large ears, as our lunarmen had, and a nose like a pipe.

We were amazed: that meant, that not only we were familiar with lunar inhabitants, but there were also other people on the Earth who had seen them. Moreover, it proved our perception. But I make this short digression only to show that we chose the proper way to walk and our feelings did not deceive us, though, of course, there could not be without mistakes.

Chapter 7

Meeting with lunar representatives

The meeting of our group with lunar representatives was appointed on Sunday. In talks Edar was a communication agent.

Four lunarmen, all of those whom Larisa had seen on the lunardrom, arrived. While our group was gathering, visitors were in the mini-ship. From the group there were only Dmitry, Natalia and Michael Fadeev, who came for the weekend from «School of phantoms» and just got to our meeting, present. Others for various reasons could not be there to take part in "symposium".

Edar appeared first and, having seen Michael, at once asked with an interest:

– "How are you getting on in study? Can you turn to phantoms?"

– "Not yet. We learn the theory, practice is ahead."

Natalia joked at once:

– "Wherefore do you attend Avdeev's school? You leave your money on the table. Do not eat for a month – and you will become a real phantom."

– "This way, most likely, I shall become a dead man rather than a phantom," - gloomy uttered Michael.

That moment a door of the mini-ship opened, guests began to go out. Anfrida first stepped on the loggia, four lunarmen followed her. They came into the room, confusedly smiling. That time they seemed a bit shy and constraining.

Best places were specially for them, i.e. a sofa and two armchairs. Our earth dwellers sat on rigid chairs and stools. Lunarmen took a seat on a sofa, Anfrida and Edar occupied armchairs. The alien just in case warned members of our group:

– "Excuse me please, but try to speak to them more softly and more politely. They have tender souls, and they feel shy in front of you."

Alexander nodded showing that everything was clear.

– "Our group is glad to meet inhabitants of the second parallel world of the Moon," - I solemnly said on behalf of the present. – "Friendship is capable to unite not only two beings, but whole worlds. Kind relations serve the best mutual understanding, bring along spiritual development and enrichment of life experience. Thank you for your time and visiting us." - and just commonly addressed that lunarman, who seemed to be the senior: - "Are you for the first time here?"

– "Yes, for the first. But other our beings go to the Earth. They have told us about people and other essences, who inhabit your parallel worlds."

– "Let they introduce themselves," - whispered to me Natalia. – "it is interesting to know their names."

– "Members of the group would like to know your names." – I addressed the same lunarman.

All of them looked very much alike each other, but despite it, at the same time there were individual distinctions between them. One had bigger mouth, another – smaller. Noses, ears, ovals of the head and expression of eyes had individual character. Therefore, if desired, they could be distinguished.

– "We are also glad to see with our own eyes inhabitants of the Earth," - said confusedly that, whom I had addressed. – "My name is Andrews-senior," – He said his name and then, having pointed to the lunarman smaller than he and sitting nearby, introduced: - "Then, this is Andrews-junior. Rostel-senior next to him and then – Rostel-junior."

– "Are these your surnames or names?"

– "Names. We are named only by names."

– "Is Andrews-junior your relative?" – asked Andrews-senior Alexander.

– "You guessed it, he is my relative," - agreed Andrews-senior. – "If your way, he is my brother, was born after me."

– "And if there are many brothers, do they have the same name?" – asked Larisa.

– "All our family is Andrews. But if there are many brothers, they vary in numbers, they are named in order of precedence: Andrews the first, the second, the third, the fourth."

– "And how about women's names?" – asked Michael.

– "We have no women. We are like your friends-aliens, - samesex."

– "Women in Space somehow play underparts," - Natalia ironically noticed. – "These aliens have no women on a planet, those – too."

– "Samesex does not mean men," – objected Michael. "Both are in one person. But it seems to me it is boring." – while his last words Anfrida came up to him and put the palm on the head. Michael felt it at once and said: - "My forehead feels hot and hair on the head began to move. What is it?"

Natalia said ironically there and then:

– "Only thinking about women makes the lover of the fair sex getting warm in brains, and makes his hair urls to allure space amazons."

Although Michael, really was the favourite of women, but had affairs only with somebody outside. He fraternized with all women in the group and did not allow anything to himself, i.e. never gave rise to more closer relations. There was brotherhood in the group, so we really never remembered that belonged to different sexes. We were united only by the general chain of knowledge.

I explained Michael's sensations:

– "Anfrida has approached you and put a hand on your head. This is a sign of approval." – And there and then addressed to Andrews-senior: - "Do you live in families?"

– "What do you mean?" - Andrews asked, confusedly smiling because did not understand what I was particularly talking about.

– "People's family is when two beings of different sexes: the man and the woman love and attract each other, live together, forming a social unit. The main thing joining them is love. But as for you, your beings are samesex. However do they live somehow together not to miss?" – I tried to explain again in terse language the complexity of mutual relations between members of a family, but felt that could not put into the explanation even ten percent of true contents of existing. If for earth dwellers two words to understand something were enough, because there were common concepts between them, that was impossible to understand for aliens, as they had another form of life.

From the Above they gave us a chance not only to learn new, but also to understand, how it was impossible sometimes to contain all those images, processes and situations, connected with a subject or phenomenon, in several short phrases. Could I really put that wealth and a subtlety of feelings peculiar to love, that variety of situations, romantic adventures or tragic moments, which form and develop family relations and feeling of love, into my explanation? It means, in those explanations given to us by the Higher during channelings, there were also hardly anything from the variety of that huge knowledge, which bear the concepts transferred by them. And therefore the latest can be developed and developed infinitely in all directions, filling them with entire scope of knowledge.

Wishing to express the word "love" as full as possible, I tried to continue an explanation.

– "Love for people has a particular value. It decorates their life. This is a big feeling …" - but further the explanation drew the line. What can you tell those, who do not understand it? How to find something common between us? But Andrews went to the rescue of me.

– "You love – means you respect each other and keep always together, don't you?"

– "Yes," - nodded I.

Each being approximated other concepts to their own. What does the concept – "respect" of two samesex beings each other hide? It sounds poorly enough, because we do not know their true relations and feelings. Therefore the cognition turned out very superficial.

– "How do your children appear?" –asked Michael.

– "The same way, as on Los and Edar's planet. They have already told you. At our end it's the same. And we are somewhat alike with them. But do not think that all beings have it identic. Many have it another way."

– "Our daughter was in your world and did not see either plants, or animals. Do you have them?"

– "No. There are only similar to us beings, and artificial forms in our world."

– "But why don't you have them?"

– "Because when it's an artificial planet they are not required," - Andrews-senior answered also confusedly and, as though excused for the negative answer. With his constrained smile he as though said that it would be more pleasant for him to answer that plants and animals were, but, unfortunately, he had to afflict us.

– "And are there animals on your planet?" – at the same time asked I the question to Edar, having remembered that we knew little about that.

– "Some plants are, but very limited quantity, and no animals at all," – answered he.

– "But your planet is alive. So then why are there no animals on it?" – I tried to understand.

– "Animals and plants are necessary to a living planet only at a certain stage of development," - explained Edar. – "When the planet becomes mature enough they are not necessary to it."

– "Do parallel worlds need plants and animals?"

– "No, there they are not necessary ... though there are also exceptions," - answered Edar.

– "Isn't it really boring to live in such empty world?"

– "We create many beautiful artificial forms, which adorn our life," - answered me Andrews-senior, as considered that their parallel world had not made on the guest from the Earth any impression.

– "How old are you?" – I addressed to lunarman.

We had to ask the same questions to compare lunar inhabitants and representatives from one of Sirius planets.

– "I am 398, it corresponds to your twenty four, and junior is 294, yours - eighteen. But your flow of time and ours are different, therefore it is impossible to compare precisely. I make an approximate comparison, only for you to understand something."

– "And what is a lifetime?"

– "From six hundred to eight hundred years. However, there are many birthdays per year."

– "How can it be?"

– "Everyone is born once, but our society has decided that it is a pleasure to celebrate it more often. Moreover, years are not added. Ten birthdays add one year."

It was not clear and incommensurable with ours, therefore I changed the topic:

– "Who governs you?"

– "We do not have leaders, we are all equal. We choose Council, and it governs. We live in peace and friendship, we are engaged in a big economy, scientific researches, power system."

– "Do your children study at special institutions, or the information is transferred to them from parents the same as on Edar's planet?"

– "There is a distinction. They have special methods of study at institutions and are engaged a lot of time in certain exercises increasing their energy. Do you know that energy exchange is very useful? You give your energy to others, and they – to you. If you leave the acquired energy to yourselves, then energetically you will stay at the same level."

– "Edar has already told us about energy exchange. But people do not pay any attention to it. They do not know that it is useful. Thus, it turns out, that you appreciate energy acquisition in development?"

– "Yes."

– "As for the person, he/she appreciates acquisition of knowledge more."

– "The man does not know yet that in Space energy is appreciated most of all. Each being should accumulate it."

– "But how?" – I asked with an interest. Our guests revealed us values about which we were completely unaware. If power increase was of some importance for the person, the use of the given process came only to improvement of a physical body.

Andrews shared his knowledge.

– "Through acquisition of high knowledge, through various terrestrial exercises the person step by step accumulates energy, too. We have heard from others that you have meditation. It can be used."

– "What's the benefit, for example, from energy increase of subtle bodies?" – asked Michael. – "When the physical body raises energy, I can lift not thirty kilograms weight, but forty. And what can I do with the energy increase of an astral body?"

— "We do not know your structure, but I'll tell another thing," - objected Andrews-senior. — "To see far away, energy of big visibility is required. It is necessary not for your material eyes. When you leave your first body, in a subtle world you will see all around using another vision. Right now, for example, you perceive only rough subjects and nothing else. But when you come out of the body, you should see around yourself other beings, which will fly everywhere, wishing to help you. So to see them, one should accumulate this special energy. The more you have, the further you will see."

So that way little by little we learnt something new from one contacts, and from another. Edar sat silently and listened to our talks with lunarmen. His eyes were full of interest, and flashed with living fire. It seemed, he was going to ask a question indeed, however left it in his mind, not disturbing lunar guests.

— "Is your civilization on the Moon big?" – asked Alexander.

— "It is much more less than yours," – continued to answer Andrews-senior. Other lunarmen only listened to us.

— "What are you doing there? What's your occupation?"

— "We work with power, adjust and maintain the energy exchange with the Earth. It is our main task. But we at the same time build, organize life, machines."

— "The American spaceship "Apollo-13" was flying to the Moon to make on its surface a small nuclear explosion for the purpose of seismic investigation. But on its way to the Moon the oxygen tank raptured. Was it an accident or deliberate actions of you?" – Alexander asked directly lunarmen.

— "Do you know about this accident?" — smiled Andrews-senior.

— "Many people heard about that failure, which the ship had met with, but what really happened, nobody knows. I think it was not an accident," - my spouse insisted.

— "Yes, you are right," - agreed Andrews. — "our services know about all intentions of people concerning the Moon. When they had known that people would like to cause moonquake and carry a bomb to us, our services flew off towards them. They remained invisible for cosmonauts and damaged their device. People must know that we will not allow to set experiments at our station."

– "But they were going to make an explosion in the material plane. Would it really have been reflected in your world?"

– "Certainly, it would necessarily have been reflected in our world. It could damage many our subtle structures. Moreover, explosion could destroy our city because the blastwave is close to the etheric world. People must know that it is impossible to interfere in what they do not understand."

– "The moon for them seems empty. They were going to carry out an experiment without any malicious intent," - I stood up for researchers. – "but we try to inform people that the Moon is alive, and any explosions are under ban there."

Our first meeting with lunarmen ended quickly. They said that designated time for Earth visit expired and it was high time to fly away, but they had a desire to meet us once again. Therefore they decided Edar would work out the issue.

We said them "thank you" for the visit, and they left us.

Michael was sitting thoughtful and sad. Natalia as usual joked:

– "Are you suffering, that lunarmen are samesex? Nobody to cut a wide swath?"

Dmitry replied at once:

– "I saw, how Anfrida was stroking the curls and looking attentively into his eyes."

– "Probably, she investigated the difference between the material visual organ and the subtle one. She is always up to the ears in researches," – declared he gloomily.

– "No, Michael, the girl was interested in you," - to chase away his sullen mood smiled Natalia. – "Don't be sad: get to know Anfrida closer. You have not girlfriends-aliens yet."

– "I am sad because cannot get into their world," - admitted the materialist. – "How can I, let me say, get acquainted with Anfrida if I do not see and hear her? It is sickening to realize my underdevelopment."

– "Are you really sad because of it?" – Natalia's eyes flashed mischievously.

– "Yes, my own juvenility gets me down. Moreover, I am sure that will study nothing practical at «School of phantoms»."

– "At the same time Anfrida sees you and understands," - tried to cheer up Natalia. – "And you feel her warmth. Thus, the contact between you is possible."

– "How can I love air? I will put her on my knees and I won't feel: she is on the left, or on the right one," - complained Michael. – "it is a pity that she is not material."

Having understood that ability to get into the subtle world was necessary more than ever, next morning he went to «School of phantoms» in Moscow.

After the meeting Anfrida unexpectedly was gone. Los came to us and with anxiety began to tell that she had flown alone by the mini-ship to a city (i.e. Moscow) to take measurements, and had to return the day before his visit, but hadn't done that.

– "First I thought that she decided to meet you on the way back," - told he, - "but, it appears, she is not here. And all of us worry about her very much."

I began to calm him down:

– "Do not worry. She is young, is simply carried away by something interesting and has forgotten about signaling. There is so much amusing in a city."

– "Do not calm me down. Don't you worry about each other? So we do. What if any dark ship will pinpoint her? We don't wish to lose her, she is darling for us. But last time she is not available. We even do not know how it has happened."

– "She does not hear so far, as you, does she?"

– "She has another structure. She can hear us only with the help of special connection. But she keeps quiet, no signals from her."

I assumed a possible place where she could be:

– "Perhaps she has decided to visit «School of phantoms». If members of our group study there, she may be interested in the process of study. Guys try to learn entering your world."

– "Are people already able to make such transition that they teach others?" – Los was surprised.

– "People are not. But one psychic is supposed to have mastered this transition and now teaches the others."

– "Is the psychic from a dark society?" – asked a counter question Los.

– "No, from the light. He teaches having good intensions. I can ring Michael up and ask whether Anfrida is there or not," - I offered my services.

– "It would be very good, if you got some information through your channels," - the alien was delighted.

Not to waste time, I began to dial the number of Moscow apartment where our companions had alighted.

Michael took the call. I told shortly what had happened and asked, whether he felt the presence of the alien.

– "No, I haven't felt any hot hugs," - he turned everything into a joke. – "Only once I saw her in my dream and that is all. I am sure, nobody has been here. Mr. Gromov at once would have noticed her with the third eye."

I passed his words along to Los.

– "So do you think, that she could go, how is it called in your language, to a rendezvous?" – He mistrustfully asked again and strictly objected: - "We will not allow. It's not the time for her. She is very young for rendezvous," - he said upbraidingly as if a severe father, and curiosity worked up again -where was Anfrida from and why did he so fatherlike worry about her.

Thoughts again began to dance in my head: «Where is the girl similar to us from? If it is a soul of a former person, why is she so clever? Her level of development is much more higher than of terrestrial contemporaries». At that moment Los continued to complain:

– "What does she keep silence? No, we cannot do nothing. So Edar has to fly to search her and immediately."

– "Please let us know when you find her," - asked Larisa. – "We worry too."

Los promised to tell us about the girl and disappeared. Fulfilling the promise, next day he appeared again and that time vigorously informed:

– "I wish to make you happy: Anfrida is found, more precisely, Edar has found her. It turns out, she carried out researches in the city and was not there, as you thought, together with your colleagues. We are glad that she has not been carried away by temptation. She couldn't inform us, as the communication device was broken."

– "We are very glad for you. Thanks for letting us know," - I thanked and then asked a new question, trying to find out something about their mutual relations as one may treat another like a friend, father, teacher. – "You worry about the girl. And how does she treat you?"

– "Very well," - assured Los. – "She respects us the same as we her. We try to help her in everything, we show her the true path, and she helps us. She is the only one here, therefore we constantly keep her out of all bad and wish her the best."

From this explanation I concluded that Los and Edar were more like her guardians.

– "I see, she is a courageous girl, if flies alone somewhere on strange planet?"

– "Yes, courageous," - agreed Los and added: - "and young," - as though emphasizing that the boldness proceeds from the youth. – "She is interested, too, in everything and would like to learn more, to get some information about the other beings, to understand how they live, what their occupations consist in ..." - After having been silent for some seconds as if remembering something, he continued: - "I wish to tell one important thing : in two full Earth rotations lunarmen will visit you. You are ready?"

– "Of course we are," - I was delighted. – "We are always glad to see them ..." - And feeling that I could hurt them with that statement, tried to mend ways. – "We are very glad to see you all. Your visits inspire us."

– "Does it mean, we have not bothered you?" – tried to find out Los.

– "Oh, don't say that! The other way round, our relations become stronger. We begin to understand each other better and better."

– "That is good, then tomorrow my colleagues and I shall visit you," - he drew a conclusion. – "Let Larisa play for us, we shall cry. Tears purify souls."

In spite of the fact that aliens refused our gifts, we constantly wanted to make their day, but could not think up what to present them. The most difficult thing was that we did not know how to transfer a thing from the material world to the subtle one. How, let us assume, to present Anfrida a brooch or some wally if she was not able even to take it, not to mention it's wearing. No doubt, Los and Edar mastered materialization, but not so that they could any material thing transfer to their world. However, that matter, as it appeared, clinched simply.

Larisa remembered that had promised Anfrida to show her clothes or as they say, the wardrobe, therefore, when three guests came, first of all she took the alien to the room and showed what terrestrial girls wore. The wardrobe was rather poor, but it was quite enough to present a terrestrial fashion to Anfrida.

While we were talking to Los and Edar in the drawing-room, Larisa laid clothes, which she considered worthy of alien's attention, in front of her and asked:

– "You always wear the only one dress. Have you got another one?"

– "We do not take in flight additional clothes. And this one we wash and disinfect. But I have one more reserve."

– "Do you feel cold in it? It's autumn outside. Does our cold get into your world?"

– "No, in our world the temperature is rather stable. I speak about the subtle world of the Earth. In it we feel neither cold, nor heat, though at the same time it's absolutely another way with your sensations in material plane. Besides, when we fly, the temperature varies in different places, for these cases we use protection, temperature regulators for our body."

– "I ask it because I would like to present you something from my clothes. But I do not know, how to do it."

Anfrida began to look attentively dresses in front of her, then pointed out one:

– "This one I like the most. Where do you take them?"

– "Usually I sew myself. But there are a lot of made up dresses in our shops. It is possible to buy them there. How about you, where do you take clothes on your planet?"

– "In special premises. However, we haven't got more than three, because others are considered unnecessary."

– "If you like this dress, please, take it," - offered the daughter. – "Perhaps Los and Edar will help you to transfer it to your world, won't they?"

– "I can do it myself," - praised herself Anfrida. "It is very easy," - and began to explain: - "You know, that each thing has also a subtle structure, the subtle body. Your material objects are based on an etheric body. If to remove it, the physical one will start to destroy. I, of course, can take an etheric body of the dress, but then the material part will quickly become inutile. Are you ready for it?"

– "Sure."

– "Right, then I shall try it on. I'm going to beg Los's permission, sometimes he shows some indulgence to me."

Anfrida first worked with a subtle body of the dress, removing it from a physical basis, and Larisa saw, how the dress as if divided into two: one remained in material world, another passed to the subtle world and became more ethereal than air. But its colour, however, changed. Then Anfrida put it on herself, and it made her appearance absolutely modern. There and then she went to the drawing-room where there were all of us, and surprised everybody very much, especially her guardians as they got used to see her in other clothes.

– "Do you like me in terrestrial dress?" – with a solemn appearance she asked the guardians.

– "You became absolutely terrestrial," – Edar paid the compliment.

Nevertheless Los did not like the comparison "terrestrial" and he corrected him:

– "Not terrestrial, but ours," - with a stress on the last word. – "the colleague from the planet 327 in a new cover."

But Anfrida did not pay attention to details of their semantic discussion, and as a truly terrestrial girl, went round in the new dress in front of everybody, walked back and forth and addressed to Los:

– "Allow me please to take it with me? Only one thing, and I will not ask something more."

Los was silent for some time, deciding what to do, then relented, seeing, that she liked it ever so much:

– "Ok. Take."

– "You can create on your planet a new terrestrial trend in outerwear," - joked Larisa.

– "Oh, we have such conservatives that it is difficult to get them moving forward. They will wear for one thousand years one dress and will be happy."

That moment an active scratching was heard outside the entrance door. Our clever and elderly enough cat named Basya came back home. Despite we lived on the third floor, it liked to take the lift and in rare cases troubled itself with natural going upstairs. When we came back home together, it «made a turn» to the lift, instead of stairs. Several times I tried to turn specially to stairs, inviting him: «Come on, let's go on foot. Do not be lazy», - but it discontentedly twitched the tail, sitting near the lift and all its appearance expressed: «What's the nonsense you are offering me. Let's go». And I had to concede its persistence. I opened lift doors, and it entered the cabin with an air of importance.

When I was absent, it usually found itself fellow travellers among neighbours, waiting for them near the lift. It waited for someone, who taking the lift and going to his/her floor, would give it lift too. Neighbours knew, what floor it lived, and gave a lift with pleasure. The cat always entered the lift first, with dignity and feeling of deal awareness.

And that moment someone brought it on the lift and it rushed home. Earlier somehow it's coming back home did not concur with aliens visit, it always walked somewhere. Now Alexander let the cat in, and their first meeting took place.

Basya entered the room. It's behaviour was anxious, it did not begin tenderly chafe feet of masters, as though showing that it was glad to see us, and wonderingly went around the room. It stopped where Los and Edar were sitting and where there was Anfrida. It came around the room several times, snuffing and twitching whiskers.

Larisa petted it and calmed:

– "It's all right, Basya."

And it lied down near her feet.

–"Who is this being? Isn't it from the society of the dark?" – Los begun to worry again, and the last question raised such laugh that I had to make great efforts to control my feelings. The others began to smile too. The analogy flashed in my head: «The man is constantly afraid of meeting with the dark, as well as they are». But answering the question, explained:

– "This is our domestic animal. It is called the cat. It is rather positive. And you, are you afraid of the dark?"

– "We are not afraid, but we do not like to meet them. There are too many troubles from them. We have heard that there are a lot of dark beings on the Earth, therefore it's better to avoid them," - explained Los, - "That's why I am asking. But in case of danger we can always neutralize them."

– "Is the cat your sacred animal?" – asked Anfrida.

– "Why do you consider that it is sacred?" - in her turn asked Larisa again.

– "You keep it in your premises. As for those, which are not sacred, I think, they are outside," - answered the girl.

– "No, cats are not sacred here," – answered Larisa. – "but people love them and keep at homes. They are tender and kind."

– "Excuse me, what is a gender of this being?" - Edar delicately enquired.

– "It is the masculine gender – a male cat," - explained Larisa. – "and there can be the feminine gender."

– "Does the feminine gender differ somehow by the appearance?" - Continued to ask Los. – "People, for example, differ at once, and it is visible with the naked eye, where the man is, and where the woman."

– "No, you will not understand cats, it is difficult to distinguish by the form," - assured Alexander. – "If to take male and female cats, you won't distinguish them."

– "Do you hint the expert is needed?" – found out Edar.

– "Yes," - nodded Alexander.

– "Could we examine it?" – Anfrida with her favourite researches at once addressed to the daughter petting the cat. – "We shall not cause it harm. It seems to us very attractive."

– "You are welcome," - agreed Larisa, completely trusting them.

Anfrida fondled his back with a hand and admired:

– "What's a soft surface."

The cat began to turn over at that time to and fro, lolling on the carpet, putting out paws and showed pleasure with all it's appearance.

– "It is lolling. Outside it is constantly in tension, there are a lot of dangers, and when it comes back home, it relaxes," - Larisa explained its behaviour.

– "What a lovely being. I like it very much," - the alien praised the cat again.

– "But it does not react for some reason to Anfrida." – noticed the daughter. – "They usually say that cats are very sensitive to alien fields. Anfrida is petting it, and it does not feel."

– "First when it entered, it reacted," - noticed I. – "Now it is playing, that's why is careless."

–"More likely, it is indifferent to my touch," - assumed the alien.

– "If the cat plays, when someone touches it, that means it enjoys the one, who does it. When they are afraid of someone, they go away," - explained Larisa.

– "Have you got some other pets or only cats?" – asked Edar.

– "As for us, we haven't, but other people keep dogs. They are larger than cats in sizes."

– "What is your domestic animal doing right now?" – addressed to Larissa Los.

The daughter began to play with it putting a pencil near it's nose and then drawing it back quickly. The cat tried to catch it and waved in air with soft paws.

– "It is playing with Larisa," - explained I. – "it takes pleasure this way."

– "Does it study something too?" – enquired about the cat Anfrida, obviously pitching an estimate of it's intelligence level too high.

– "No, the cat understands nothing. It's mind has a low degree of development," - answered Alexander.

– "Why do you think so? It just understands everything very well," – Edar, attentively observing the cat, unexpectedly went to bat for it. – "and it should feel us, if sets itself up to it."

– "It understands good, but to think, like the person, is not capable," - Alexander began to explain, why he called the cat "not thinking" being. — "Everything concerning it's interests, it perfectly understands, but is not capable to think over. And also it cannot create, make something new."

— "It's clear," - Edar nodded, staring at the cat. Then it took out of his overalls pocket some device, went up to Basya and sat down before it. Anfrida and he began to examine.

At first the cat laid calmly, spreadeagle, on the carpet, holding pads up, then listened to itself and with a puzzled look lifted up a head, trying to understand, where those sensations came from. The mistress did not touch it, she stood nearby, but something bothered it. Visible bewilderment was reflected in its green eyes as well as misunderstanding the origin of its sensations.

Anfrida petted its side, then belly, and Edar put a device to various sites of a body. Basya nervously began to twitch ears, feeling that something happened. But when Edar set a device on it's head between ears, its sight became as though mad, reflecting full misunderstanding of the case. It jumped up and rushed headlong to daughter's room. It hid there behind a sofa and did not appear any more till the end of the evening.

— "He is afraid of you," - Alexander explained its behaviour. — "as you can see, the cat perfectly feels you."

Seeing that researches had finished, Edar asked Larisa to play earthly melodies. The evening ended on a lyrical note. Aliens listened attentively, thoughtfully and everyone in his/her own way.

Chapter 8

Parting

We made preparations for the following meeting with lunar inhabitants in depth. We prepared many souvenirs, as considered, if aliens from the planet 327 did not want to take anything, it might be possible to present lunarmen and, thereby, to show that inhabitants of the Earth were capable not only of aggression, but also of good. We would like to show best side of mankind. Although we understood that lunarmen like Edar and Los did not eat terrestrial food, however we put on a table plates with fruit, lighted three candles there, switched on Christmas fairy lights on walls. Together with lights we also hanged balloons. The room looked gaily decorated, celebratory.

As usual we waited for them from the loggia outside, but they, out of the blue appeared from above, thus that time they passed through slabs of the nine-floor building, going down to our, third floor.

There were five lunarmen. As always, Los, Edar, Anfrida and our family were there too. Nobody from the group had come. Some people continued their study at «School of phantoms», others that day as appeared were busy for various reasons. Thus, our family was, as they say, face to face with the visitors. But, probably, it was specially planned so from the Above.

Guests took vacant seats.

– "Hello, our dear paternalized," - addressed to us Los truly in an earthly way and applied with regard to us the word "paternalized". Obviously, as earth dwellers were below them, if to compare the level of development, he decided that they patronized their younger co-brothers. – "Meeting with you gives all of us a great pleasure," - continued he. – "our stay on your planet is filled with a special sense. It is for the first time when earth dwellers come in friendly contact with such a number of various beings. And we do hope it will serve as the beginning of their warm relations with all beings of the Space."

– "We welcome on behalf of earth dwellers our guests," - in tone to him solemnly answered I. – "we are glad and consider it an honor that you paid us this visit. As a special sign of favour to all those present we wish to hand over you small souvenirs. Larisa and I have made them ourselves. This is a symbol of an orthodox cross made of beads, it is a symbol of belief in Higher Spirit," - I put into symbols those concepts, which were acceptable for their understanding. – "The pendant "heart" symbolizes love and mutual respect." – while speaking, I took up and showed pendants. –"And here are necklaces «terrestrial flowers». Let they be a remembrancer to you about our blue planet. We want our Earth leave only kind memory. There are three types of souvenirs, thus total twelve. So much for everyone. Please choose, what you like."

– "We thank you for a warm greeting," - on behalf of the guests answered Los and for the first time did not refuse to take souvenirs. – "I wish to introduce you one more lunarman – Yarsel. He is from the Council of lunar contacts," - Los pointed out the newcomer. He smiled.

– "It is a great pleasure to see the interest to our small collective of such … persona," - feeling the lack of space terminology knowledge I was confused for some seconds, therefore I had to use an old word. – "A circle of our invisible friends has extended. People consider that they are alone in Space. But if you are from the Council of contacts, then you likely will answer such a question: Are there any material beings on nearby planets? And why are there more invisible beings than visible?" – I addressed directly to Yarsel.

– "Of course, are," - assured he. – "Do not think that people are unique as the material form of life evidence. And there are forms similar to yours on other planets. The material body is temporary for you, and through some stage of development people, too, will pass into other phase and become invisible to other material beings. And as for the question who is more: material or subtle, nobody can give the exact answer to you, because nobody of us has seen the Universe border."

In Yarsel's speech one could feel power and knowledge of a great scope of information.

– "What civilizations do you know, besides the Earth and the planet 327?" – asked I.

– "Those, which are technically highly developed, have powerful flying machines and fly to many neighboring planets. But there are also material forms, which cannot be called alive basing on your way of understanding. They are as though completely merged with the material nature. We know that many people do not believe in our existence, but it is because they know very little about Space life. The man should be given new knowledge to create other ideology standing above the present one."

– "How about you to look after mankind and help it to broaden the space mind," - offered Alexander.

– "We have noticed that people always hope for someone's help, but they should hope only for themselves. Everything depends on them, on acceleration of their development. The help in affairs or in something else coming from higher alien civilizations will harm people only because they cannot adequately manage new knowledge. High knowledge should find worthy ideology, morals. Only in this case they can be oriented to good, instead of harm."

– "And you personally, could you give something useful to mankind?" - Alexander could not calm.

– "Yes, we could much, but we shall not give, because people are very unruly in their behaviour. Preliminary contacts with the Earth have shown that people are not ready yet to get the brotherly help from those, who are elder, if to compare mind. They will simply destroy themselves by new knowledge. Knowledge is given for the good, but the person turns it to harm suchlike. Therefore the Space does not interfere in terrestrial affairs till some time. Learn first how to turn into the good. Be aware that any interference in another destiny always leaves consequences. It is necessary to remember it."

– "But is there any neutral knowledge, which would help in development and cause no harm to the man?" – asked I.

– "It was checked not one time, that even safe knowledge the person is capable to turn into harm. You give to the person something good, and at once their opponents appear, thus struggle between them begins. You have constant conflicts. And the reason of it is an insufficient level of development and immorality."

– "But how about you, do you have morals indeed?" – I asked, remembering that they were samesex and thinking, that there were no morals at their end.

– "We have a discipline and strict abidance by development laws. Laws should provide development of each member of society, instead of protecting interests of a small group of some beings," - firmly declared Yarsel.

I noticed that our guests were bored. They were not, probably, interested in a serious topic of conversation, as they knew it since long ago, and we made a discovery just that moment. We had to change the topic and make it more interesting to the others. But, as they say, the closer to life, the more interesting to the majority would be, and I decided to turn conversation to simple questions, moreover, the difficult ones could not make the destiny of mankind better.

– "Inhabitants of the Earth call themselves, when there are a lot of them, earth dwellers. And how are inhabitants of the Moon called?"

– "This is a question of my Level," - Andrews-senior entered conversation. – "Please, allow me to answer."

It seemed they classified all questions by the level of their complexity, and every lunarman answered that, which corresponded its development rate.

– "You are welcome", - agreed I.

My question was for Yarsel, but it didn't matter who would answer it. However I paid attention that as I had passed to more simpler questions, only Andrews-senior began to answer me further. Obviously, there were certain rules of behaviour in their etiquette. And it explained the case, when seniors were speaking, the others were silent.

– "We call ourselves similarly to earthmen – lunarmen."

– "We have found out, there is no division into men and women in your civilization. But some people on the Earth met lunar fairies. Who are these beings and where are they from? Or is it a human imagination?"

– "Yes, they exist in the third parallel world of the Moon. These are special beings. There are very few of them. They, too, are samesex. They are guardians of kindness. You know, the word "fairy" means in lunar understanding "kind". They sometimes help us. It happens on the Earth they also help to your earth dwellers. They have such mission – to help."

– "Have you met them, as us?" – Larisa asked with an interest.

– "Yes. But they fly only voluntarily, not taking into consideration our desires. They do not have flying machines or any ships for moving. They fly in the body."

– "It is possible to fly in the body from one world to another if the worlds belong to one planet," - agreed Larisa. – "And is it possible to fly without a spaceship, too, from planet to planet?"

– "Yes, but for this purpose it is necessary to reach a certain level of development. Fairies have such level, therefore they visit your world, and ours without ships. But we, unfortunately, have to use equipment for a while," - complained Andrews-senior.

– "The question is as follows. The Moon has no own atmosphere, does it matter for you?" – asked I.

– "Why do you think, that it hasn't?"

– "I mean the material world."

– "No, in this plane it has no value for us, because we are constructed for our subtle world, for our atmosphere."

– "When I visited your world, I saw far away high-rise buildings. Does it mean, you live similarly to us?" –asked Larisa.

– "We call them not buildings, but premises," - corrected Andrews. – "They are alike with yours by their type and have high-speed moving inside. For example, you are at the first level, and then at once move up to the tenth."

– "In our language it is a lift," – suggested them the terrestrial term Larisa.

– "You have the lift, and on the Moon it is called «a room of high-speed movement»."

– "Tell us please, what is the sense of existence for you? What for do you live?" – asked unexpectedly for them the daughter.

I say "unexpectedly", because they hesitated with their reply, there was an awkward pause, then Yarsel answered again. Obviously, they determined the level of the question and the one, who had to answer.

– "We were created by the Higher. We are obliged to Them and that's why should pass properly that way, which They determined for us. The way is difficult, but necessary for our development. It is the same, as you have. We live for the sake of progress and for the sake of progress of the Higher, because everything is interconnected. They depend on us as well as we depend on Them."

– "Human development is based on knowledge about the world and struggle with desires. What's the basis of your development? Do you struggle with your desires?" – I was interested.

– "Our progress is based similarly on comprehension of the new. We have acquired very well that it is impossible to cling to the old, otherwise it will lead you to the deadlock. But at the same time the new without the old will be too fragile and breakable. Therefore in perception we build a chain, which joins constantly the old to the new. We have desires too, but they are different. Some of them help to move ahead and accumulate energy of the soul, others pull back as the power goes down because of them. And our representatives overcome such desires, suppress them inside. It is important only to be able to determine what brings along progression, and what leads to regression. We try to work hard and suppress low desires."

– "Then what low desires do you have? What can tempt you?" – asked Larisa.

– "Certainly, there are no such temptations in our world as on the Earth," - began to answer again Andrews. – "our inhabitants do not play cards, are not poisoned with gas from tubules (he meant cigarettes), we do not have women, we are samesex. You have drinks, we haven't."

– "But you have just told that can be tempted with something and lose energy because of it. What have you meant exactly?" – asked to give details Alexander.

– "Our temptations are of another kind," - said Andrews. – "for example, you would like to do something simple, which gives you nothing for development. Sometimes you would like to have a rest, lie around and slug. This is number one. Another thing is that you would like simply, without purpose, fly spaceships. It is a big expense of energy as energy is used not only by a ship, but by us too. It is for us a temptation. We struggle with them."

– "Can you influence the destiny?" – was interested Alexander.

– "Roughly speaking, we think, as you. We try to do only good, because our actions, first of all, are reflected on our future. Is it clear for you?"

– "Yes, it is,"- confirmed Alexander.

– "When a being causes someone harm," - continued Andrews-senior, - "first of all, it causes it to itself."

– "The human has five senses: vision, sense of hearing, sense of smell, sense of touch, sense of taste. And how many senses do you have?" – I addressed to Andrews.

– "We have a bit more. For example, we can feel the energy necessary to us at a very big distance. Moreover, we know what will happen to us in the nearest future. We do not know how it is called in your language. For example, you fly the ship, and there should be something bad with you soon," - he began to explain, – "and you have already felt it."

– "Intuition," – suggested Alexander.

– "Yes, our intuition works very well. But it is sensitized not only to bad, but also to good. We have flied to you with a great joy, because have felt that you receive us very good. And we were not mistaken. We like the way you have decorated the room, you have presented to us souvenirs and have cheered us up by all of these. We see, how terrestrial beings live there and can compare with ours. You gave us many pleasant moments, but, unfortunately, it is time to come back. We thank you for cordial welcome. We will bring with ourselves the best memoirs about you."

They said goodbye and one after another began to go upwards, passing through slabs. We stayed all three. We sat thoughtfully in our seats for some time.

– "Hey, did they take souvenirs?" - remembered Larisa and went up to a shelf on which they were. It was empty there. All souvenirs disappeared. – "Well done," - the daughter was delighted, - "they took." – she returned to an armchair and addressed to us: - "Have you seen, when they have taken and what way?"

– "No," – we shook heads. – "Nobody has noticed anything."

– "They have simply disappeared and that's all. How do materialization and dematerialization occur?" – Deliberated aloud the daughter.

– "If you live so many years, as they do, you will know," - thoughtfully answered Alexander.

– "Evolution proves, the longer you live, the more you can," - reworded I.

We were sitting thoughtfully, not clear for what reason, as if we were waiting for something. The intuition, probably, came into action. Suddenly Anfrida appeared in the room again.

– "I have returned," - she said. – "while they are bringing lunarmen, I shall sit with you. I have seen lunarmen many times. They look like Los. And I am just another. It seems to me, I am the same, as Larisa. I do not understand only, why is she material and I am etheric?"

We, too, did not understand it and could not answer her question.

– "Do you know something about your origin?" – cautiously asked I.

– "No. They do not tell me. They are kidding that have found me on a mysterious planet Anfrida and named after it. But I see that I look like earthly girls."

– "It is not important in what form to be, the main thing is that there are loving beings near to you. Edar and Los respect you very much and worry, when you get lost somewhere," - I tried to dispose her properly and to dispel unnecessary doubts.

– "Did they worry very much, when I flied to a city?" – She asked again.

– "Yes, very much," - confirmed I, the others nodded in sign of consent.

It consoled her and gladdened.

– "That means, they are not indifferent to me. They call me colleague and only colleague," - discontent was heard in her tone. – "but I have a question to Larisa. While there are no Edar and Los, I wish to ask her something about so-called men," - and she kept silence for some time.

The pause was meaningful, and Alexander understood, if they started talking about men, he should leave women alone, therefore he came out of the room.

Anfrida addressed to us:

– "It is interesting for me to know, how do you treat the male? Respectfully or with contempt?"

– "As for me I divide only into good and bad," - answered Larisa. – "I do not respect bad. I am kind to good, whatever appearance they have."

– "Los and Edar said to me, that one should treat decently the malicious. You can be angry at them. But outwardly do not demonstrate feelings and then it will be better to you."

– "They are right," – confirmed I. – "Norms of high morals are the same everywhere. The higher the being, the better it should treat everybody."

– "If to show bad beings outwardly discontent, you will play the devil," - continued to argue Anfrida. – "And in general, do you consider men equal to or lower than you?"

I decided to answer that question.

– "Every person, of course, has his/her own opinion. But personally I consider them equal. However, sometimes you can meet very clever among them. The male mind surpasses the female one. Scientists, engineers are basically men. But women surpass them in other qualities – kindness, love, tenderness. The difference is in availability of these or those qualities."

– "But when two different halves join, they achieve big results in life if respect each other. Do you agree with it?" – expressed her thoughts Anfrida.

Obviously, counting herself similar to us, she shared with us what could not share neither with Los, nor with Edar, as, despite their unisexuality, she felt in them something alien.

– "Yes," - we confirmed.

– "I would like also to get acquainted with the opposite sex of my age, but from terrestrial ones," - admitted the alien. – "it is necessary only that he would be like me. Material men do not hear me. I tried to talk to your Michael in a city, but he does not perceive me."

– "Are you into him?" – asked Larisa.

– "Yes," – confessed open-heartedly the alien.

I pondered how to help and how could they meet or hear each other? And suddenly it came to me in a flash. I offered to Anfrida:

– "You can meet him in the subtle world, at the moment of his death. He will leave the material world, his soul will fly out in a subtle body, then grasp him, put him in the ship and go to your planet. Only you should wait first when he will live his life and die of old age. However the soul remains eternally young, he will fly out younger, than you have just seen him. The only point is that you have to wait, but I think, it's not a problem. You live long, and to wait for some sixty years for you is a trifle."

– "Will he agree to fly with me?" – The girl began to doubt.

– "He loves adventures."

– "It is a good idea," - Anfrida was delighted. – "I will necessarily wait. By this time Los and Edar will have stoped to consider me too young. I will have a friend, and we will fly together the ship," - she was lost in day dreams at once. – "I shall show him a lot of interesting things on other planets. But first I have to go away to our planet and when he will be eighty years old, I'll be back for him."

Anfrida left us full of iridescent hopes. But the hour of parting draws near.

Our aliens had to depart ahead of time, without having finished all researches on the Earth. In a week three of them appeared with sad news.

– "The message has come, our planet has been attacked again. All ships are called back," - informed Los. – "We must leave the Earth. We are sad to part with you. We have never left other planets with such regret, as yours. Usually you fly back home rapidly with the desire to see relative beings sooner. But this time it is hard for us to part with beings from another planet."

Edar slowly came closer to Larisa. His face reflected grief.

– "I am bringing away your wonderful music in my soul to other beings. Your earthly melodies will sound on our planet. I will remember you each time unit of my existence." – his big eyes reflected sadness. – "It's for the first time when my soul is torn between two planets. I shall remember you forever."

– "And I shall remember another person most of all," - mysteriously said Anfrida, but we had already known whom exactly she was talking about. – "Everyone of us leaves here own particle.

Therefore, when the war will end, we altogether shall necessarily come to you," – promised the alien.

We were sad too. The reason of sadness was that we came to love beings from the planet 327, and did not want to part with them.

Los went up to us and offered one hand to Alexander, another to me purely in a terrestrial way.

– "I concentrate energy to make our handshake ardent," - he said. – "I thank you for pleasant time, which we have spent together. We have received from you a lot of new and interesting information. On our way home we shall process it, and then start studying. I do hope, we also have helped you to look into things which are not present in your world."

I felt, how heat went to my palm from his hand. Concentration of energy occurred normally. It was the only way of feeling each other. It was a handshake between two worlds, handshake from one dimension to another. But it bore warmth of souls and good.

They flew away, but that warmth remained to burn the fire of hope for our new meeting in the future.

*　　*　　*

Afterword

Many people will take this story for a phantom of authors' imagination as the events here seem too incredible. However it is the documentary book about the events, which have taken place during our work with subtle planes.

In our books I describe events occurred only till 1993. All the rest, I mean our way from 1993 till 2000, I leave under seal of secrecy. It is just for the initiated.

But we give everyone an opportunity to follow us in rising to Divine Heights, and offer new knowledge for this in all our books. Everybody's way will be individual, but every person through study of the knowledge sent by God can reach a space consciousness, which opens gates to the Divine Hierarchy.

*   *   *

The books of «Beyond the Bounds of Unknown» series

Authors: Larisa Seklitova, Ludmila Strelnikova

«The Soul and Secrets of its Structure»
«Secrets of the Higher worlds»
«Unordinary Life of Heavenly Teachers»
«Energy Structure of the Man and the Matter»
«The Higher Mind Reveals the Secrets»
«Rendezvous with the Invisibles»
«Creation of Forms or Experiments of the Higher Mind»
«The Life in Someone Else's body»
«The Man of Aquarius Epoch»
«Pearls of the Higher Truths»
«Glossary of the Cosmos Philosophy»
«Philosophy of Eternity»
«Philosophy of the Absolute»
«Personality and Eternity»
«Development of the Soul or Paradoxical Philosophy» 1,2.
«Laws of Macrocosm or the Basis of Heavenly Hierarchy Subsistence» 1, 2.
«Matrix as the Basis of the Soul».
«The Finger of Fate»
«New Model of Macrocosm, or the Secret of the Universe revealed»
«Terrestrial and eternal» (answers to questions)
«Prometheus's Fire or Mysticism in Our Life»

Authors Alexander Strelnikov, Ludmila Strelnikova

«Space Revelations»
«Talks about the Unknown»

«Magic of perfection» series.

«Freedom and Destiny».
«Karmic lessons of Fate»
«Phenomenon of the Soul or how to reach perfection»
«Great Transition or Versions of the Apocalypse»

«Esoteric in maxims»series

Books:
«Diamond Panes»
«Lotus Petals»
«Star Blues»
«Mirror of Wisdom»
«Sonata of Truth»
«Ode of Eternity»
«Wisdom in maxims».

Larisa Aleksandrovna Seklitova
Ludmila Leonovna Strelnikova

RENDEZVOUS WITH THE INVISIBLES